Preparing Research Articles

P O C K E T   G U I D E S   T O
SOCIAL WORK RESEARCH METHODS

Series Editor
Tony Tripodi, DSW
Professor Emeritus, Ohio State University

Determining Sample Size:
Balancing Power, Precision, and Practicality
Patrick Dattalo

BRUCE A. THYER

Preparing
Research
Articles

OXFORD
UNIVERSITY PRESS

2008

OXFORD

UNIVERSITY PRESS

Oxford University Press, Inc., publishes works that further
Oxford University's objective of excellence
in research, scholarship, and education.

Oxford   New York
Auckland   Cape Town   Dar es Salaam   Hong Kong   Karachi
Kuala Lumpur   Madrid   Melbourne   Mexico City   Nairobi
New Delhi   Shanghai   Taipei   Toronto

With offices in
Argentina   Austria   Brazil   Chile   Czech Republic   France   Greece
Guatemala   Hungary   Italy   Japan   Poland   Portugal   Singapore
South Korea   Switzerland   Thailand   Turkey   Ukraine   Vietnam

Published by Oxford University Press, Inc.
198 Madison Avenue, New York, New York 10016

www.oup.com

Oxford is a registered trademark of Oxford University Press

Library of Congress Cataloging-in-Publication Data
Thyer, Bruce A.
Preparing research articles / Bruce A. Thyer.
p. cm.—(Pocket guides to social work research methods)
Includes bibliographical references and index.
ISBN-13: 978-0-19-532337-5 (pbk. : alk. paper)
1. Sociology—Authorship—Handbooks, manuals, etc.
2. Sociology—Research—Handbooks, manuals, etc.
3. Report writing—Handbooks, manuals, etc.   I. Title.
HM569.T49 2008
808'.0663—dc22
2007037947

Acknowledgments

All of us are shaped by our environments, physical and interpersonal. I can trace back the genesis of this book to almost 30 years ago, when I began my PhD studies in the joint Doctoral Program in Social Work and Social Science at the University of Michigan. The University of Michigan School of Social Work was headed by Dean Philip Fellin, and the Doctoral Program was directed by Professor Yeheskel (Zeke) Hazenfeld. The social work faculty, whom I was fortunate to be able to receive instruction from, included Edwin Thomas, Tony Tripodi, David Himle, Sheila Feld, Norma Radin, Jack Rothman, and Charles Garvin, while in psychology I learned from luminaries such as Hazel Markus, Robert Zajonc, James McConnell, and Richard Nisbett. My major professor was a psychologist named James Papsdorf, who was incredibly supportive, and a wonderful psychiatrist over in the Department of Psychiatry named George Curtis proved to be an ideal clinical and research mentor, as were my psychiatric colleagues Oliver Cameron and Randolph Nesse. My tolerant and much appreciated clinical social work supervisor was David Neale. While I would not want any of these colleagues to be blamed for my professional missteps over the past 30 years, I would like to acknowledge the positive instrumental role that they played in my professional development. I am most grateful to them and to my Doctoral Program. I dedicate this book to two other important influences in my professional life, Alisa Rosenbaum and Friedrich A. Hayek.

Bruce A. Thyer
Tallahassee, FL

Contents

Preparing Research Articles

1

The Importance of Journal Articles

In professional and scientific fields such as social work, the publication of an article in a high-quality peer-reviewed journal is viewed as a contribution to disciplinary knowledge that stands somewhat above other forms of scholarship. Why is this? Is it fair? Should this epistemological privileging of certain ways of disseminating research over others be endorsed and supported by you and the profession at large? In this initial chapter, I review the status of research articles as a form of professional contribution in social work, and I try to explain the rationale for valuing such articles over other ways of contributing to knowledge in the field. In later chapters I discuss considerations regarding locating and selecting an appropriate journal to submit your work to; how to prepare and submit your research manuscript; and your obligations as an author after your manuscript has been submitted, accepted, and published. My intent is to help clear away some of the mysteries, or at least little-understood processes, of publishing research articles, and to enhance your success in that area. In turn, I (perhaps immodestly) hope that the general field of social work scholarship will be enhanced. I have accrued some of this information(at times painfully) by working as a moderately successful researcher myself, by serving on the editorial boards of various social work and non–social work journals, by authoring and editing some social work research books, and by editing one reasonably well-regarded social work research journal for some 18 years. I have made many mistakes and have had some successes. By conveying these experiences to you, perhaps I will enable you to better evade the former and promote the latter.

The next section outlines some reasons for why the authorship of articles in peer-reviewed journals is accorded greater distinction.

The Peer-Review Process

Most professional social work journals have adopted the publication style developed by the American Psychological Association and described in a very important reference book called the *Publication Manual of the American Psychological Association* (American Psychological Association [APA], 2001), as have journals in a wide array of disciplines in the behavioral and social sciences. In addition to requiring that manuscripts submitted to a given journal be physically formatted in APA style, most social work journals have also adopted a process to aid them in the selection of articles for publication; this process is called "peer review" and is also outlined in the APA style manual. Briefly (and discussed in a later chapter in greater detail), manuscripts are submitted to a journal's editor (or editor-in-chief). He or she sends the author (i.e., you) a postcard, a postally mailed letter, or an e-mail acknowledging receipt of the paper and assigns the work a number for future correspondence purposes. The editor invites two or more individuals with some background in the subject matter of your paper to read it. These reviewers may be members of the journal's formal editorial board, or they may be guest reviewers selected for their specialized expertise. Before it is sent out for review, all identifying information (name, institutional affiliation, etc.) is removed from your submission. The reviewers are thus "blind" when they critique your work. This helps guard against gender bias or chances of the institution you are with (say, the

University of Michigan, which has a highly prestigious social work program, versus, say, Rustic State U., of lesser distinction) biasing the reviewers' appraisal.

In due course the editor receives several reviews of your paper, each of which will, apart from providing a narrative qualitative and quantitative critique, recommend that it be accepted for publication, revised by you and resubmitted for further review, or rejected. Revised articles resubmitted to the editor may or may not be subjected to further review by the original reviewers (or others). Many journals simply have the editor evaluate the extent to which your revision satisfactorily addresses the reviewers' suggestions, and the editor alone then accepts or rejects the work.

It is widely held that selecting articles for publication in this manner, using blind peer review, is superior to alternative methods, and this is why almost all journals in social work use blind peer review. And it is this element of constructive critical appraisal and (usually) suggestions for revision by presumptive experts on your paper's topic that elevates the article selected for publication in peer-reviewed journals above other contributions to disciplinary scholarship. There have been a couple of empirical studies evaluating the merits of using blinded versus nonblinded reviewers (that is, reviews in which the author's identity is either masked or not), and according to them blind review did not seem to enhance the quality of the reviews or the time of processing reviews to medical journals (e.g., Justice, Cho, Winker, Berlin, & Rennie, 1998; van Rooyen, Godlee, Evans, Smith, & Black, 1998). And to be honest, I am not aware of any controlled evaluations empirically demonstrating that articles chosen for publication on the basis of peer review are of higher quality than articles published in journals either that are open-access (meaning they accept pretty much everything that is submitted to them) or whose editor is solely responsible for selecting which ones to accept, without any peer-review mechanism. But even absent such data, it is almost axiomatic in the research communities of all disciplines that article selection via peer review enhances the quality of what is published.

Journals Are Superior Vehicles for Disseminating your Findings

Your research and findings are valuable to the scientific community only to the extent that other scholars are able to come into contact with your work. An article published in a quality peer-reviewed journal will appear in the hard-copy issues of the journal received by individuals and libraries that subscribe to that journal. Articles are also increasingly Internet accessible through Web sites maintained by the publishers of journals, through institutional libraries that have an electronic subscription to the journal, and through various databases and indexing services. Nowadays, anyone wishing to find out what a given person has authored can simply insert that person's name into a search engine (e.g., PsycInfo, *Web of Science*), and *voilà*—an up-to-date list of the articles that person has authored will appear. Most major university libraries now grant faculty and students (and sometimes alumni) access to complete copies of articles published in journals subscribed to by that university. What this means pragmatically is that an article appearing in a journal that supports a concurrent or slightly delayed electronic version of each issue is almost instantly available to anyone with Internet access. Your journal article has a near worldwide audience.

Books and book chapters do not, as yet, possess this level of ease of accessibility; hence, as a means of disseminating your research, the journal article is head and shoulders above these other two means of conveying information. Presentations at local, state, regional, national, and international conferences are typically made to a relatively small audience, whose members may dutifully pick up the hard copy of the paper or PowerPoint presentation you offer them; with the exception of those hardy souls who actually heard you at the conference, though, most other folks with an interest in your topic will have no practical way of coming into contact with your work. Very few conferences publish complete "proceedings," or contents of all papers presented at that meeting, and those that are published tend to consist of many pages of dissimilarly formatted papers photocopied and bound, with little careful editing. Some conferences make their papers available on DVD, or even on the Web, but this is rare, and the careful editing and proofing associated with the publication of a journal article is usually lacking. Also, many conferences have a very high acceptance rate for submitted proposals. Part of the reason for this is simply that conferences are a success only if people attend them, and the more papers they accept, the more folks pay to attend the conference. Some international conferences have exceedingly high acceptance rates, as do some national specialty social work conferences in the United States. This is another reason why papers published in high-quality journals that use a selective peer-review system have greater prestige than research papers presented at conferences.

Journals Are Quicker

In many fields, speed is of the essence: the sooner a new discovery is communicated to the professional community, the better. Much social work research lacks this element of time pressure. While we of course want our work to emerge in print sooner rather than later, this is usually not due to our fears that someone will "scoop" our discovery or beat us to the punch (unlike some fields, such as high-energy physics). While there is variation, of course, it usually takes a shorter time period for an article to move from initial submission into print than it does for a book or book chapter. Some of the very best science journals can move submitted papers from review to acceptance and into print in a couple of months, but no social work journal has this expeditious a publication mechanism in place. About 1 year is the fastest that the best of the social work journals can move in this regard, and some are quite slow. In a survey of authors who had published an article in a social work journal, we found that some journals took as long as 2 years to inform authors that their article had been accepted (Thyer & Myers, 2003)! This is inexcusably long. I had the Winter 2007 issue of the *Journal of Social Work Education* at hand as I wrote this book, and I found that the first article in that issue had been accepted in September 2004 (a 27-month lag), the second article had been accepted in March 2005 (almost a 2-year lag), the third in July 2005 (over 18 months), etc. As sadly slow as this process often is, though, it is usually speedier than moving a completed book manuscript through the steps of submission, acceptance, typesetting, production, and publication. Hence, for reasons of both dissemination and speed, journal articles are preferable over other models of communication.

Promotion and Tenure Decisions Within Academic Social Work

Nowadays, the modal model for a social work faculty member is someone who has earned the MSW degree or its equivalent (e.g., MSSW, MSSA, MA) from a program accredited by the Council on Social Work Education (CSWE); has several years of practice experience; and has earned a PhD in social work or a closely related field such as psychology, education, sociology, political science, etc. These folks typically are hired into a tenure-earning position as assistant professors. They will usually spend 5 to 7 years as an assistant professor and then apply for promotion to the higher rank of associate professor, at which time they will be awarded tenure. "Tenure" means that a faculty member can be dismissed only for cause (e.g., consistently bad teaching, substance abuse problems, abusing students, committing a felony), and even then only after a prolonged review process, complete with suitable venues for appeal. It does not mean that one has a job for life or that one cannot be fired.

When applying for promotion and tenure (P & T), one usually prepares a P & T dossier, a compilation of one's accomplishments in the areas of teaching, research, and service during one's appointment as an assistant professor. The variables used to document one's research achievements include such things as copies of articles that have been published in peer-reviewed journals, manuscripts of articles that have been formally accepted but not yet printed, published or in-press book chapters, edited books, authored books, and other lesser bits of evidence of one's scholarship. Included here are things such as book reviews; editorials; prefaces; letters or comments appearing in professional journals; and papers delivered at state, regional, national, or international conferences. Surveys have been undertaken asking academic faculty and administrators to rank these various forms of scholarship, and in social work, as in most disciplines, having authored an article that was published in a peer-reviewed journal is seen as the highest, most creditable evidence of scholarship, relative to the other indicators mentioned above. Within this broad category, varying amounts of credit are given for being sole author (higher credit) versus one of a series of authors (lesser credit), first of a series of authors (higher) versus being farther down in the list of authors (lower), having an article appear in a higher-quality journal versus a lower-quality journal, lengthier articles versus brief ones, articles containing sophisticated statistical analyses of collected empirical data (higher) versus a secondary analysis of data originally gathered by others or one that uses less complex inferential tools (lesser).

Seipel (2003) conducted a survey study using a random sample of 189 social work faculty employed at programs offering the MSW or the MSW and PhD degrees. The survey addressed the relative importance of various types of publications, and Seipel found empirical support for many of the opinions mentioned above. Here are some illustrative quotes from this report:

- "[P]eer-reviewed work should be given the greatest weight for tenure consideration . . . the respondent's ratings for peer-reviewed publications were from one third to one half greater in value than their ratings for non-peer-reviewed publications . . . social work educators who are beginning their careers should work towards publishing in peer-reviewed or critically-juried publications" (pp. 81–82).
- "[A] single-authored publication was given the highest value of any form of authorship" (p. 83).
- "Beginning social work educators should strive to be a sole author, or the first author of a collaborative project" (p. 84).
- "[P]ublishing an empirical paper was slightly more valuable for tenure considerations than publishing non-empirical work" (p. 85).

The above guidelines are very general indeed; of course individual social work programs may choose to emphasize some contributions over others, and indeed individual senior faculty (e.g., those with tenure) appraising P & T dossiers may apply their own preferences at variance with those officially endorsed by their program. But be that as it may, these guidelines, fair or not, are those most commonly endorsed within academic social work, and their existence is a pragmatic reality that faculty aspiring to promotion should take into account in calculating their chances for being promoted.

Hasn't the Internet Made Print Journals Outmoded?

Far from it. In fact, contrary to the seemingly gleeful prognostications made by Internet enthusiasts a decade ago of the demise of hard-copy publications, the Internet has dramatically increased the impact of hard-copy journals! Two concurrent developments have brought this about. Gimlet-eyed commercial publishers, with so much financial and human capital invested in their stable of print journals—journals from which they reap immense profits—are not about to let their golden goose escape. What they have done is make available Web-based versions of their print journals, parallel with the publication of the hard-copy version. Individual subscribers now are often provided with a choice— buy a print subscription, which will be mailed to them; buy a *lower-cost* Internet subscription, which is often available a few weeks prior to the appearance of the print version; or buy a concurrent subscription, one that provides a hard copy of each issue and concurrent access to a Web-based version. The Web-based versions are a win–win for the publishers. Internet publication of a journal costs very little, far less than producing a print version. Publishers have no printing or mailing costs associated with their online subscriptions. The articles were being set up in camera-ready PDF (portable data file) format anyway, as part of the hard-copy production process, so making PDFs of each issue available online for a subscription fee is a pretty easy way to earn additional income.

Many social workers continue to prefer to read a research article from a hard-copy journal rather than from a computer monitor. You can make annotations on the printed page, use a yellow highlighter, underline sentences, etc., and having a row of journals neatly aligned on one's office bookshelf is validation that one is truly a legitimate scholar! If you have only an electronic subscription, it can be hard to access articles while, say, on the beach (plus, sand can get into your drive slots). Frankly, nothing beats relaxing in a hammock strung between two palm trees and sipping a frozen daiquiri while perusing the latest, exciting hard-copy issue of your favorite journal. Unexpectedly, the revenues afforded by Internet subscriptions have, paradoxically, supported the existence of print journals in the face of rising production and mailing costs.

Another factor contributing to the perpetuation of the print journal has been the revenue-enhancing practice of "bundling." Let's take a major publisher such as SAGE Publications, which produces over 450 print journals, including the one I edit, *Research on Social Work Practice (RSWP)*. A single subscription to this journal currently costs a library about $430 a year. That seems like a lot, but keep in mind that an individual subscriber is charged only $130, and anyone joining the Society for Social Work and Research (www.sswr.org) for $100 a year can get a free subscription to the journal as a membership benefit at no additional cost. Say the university library has noted that *RSWP* is used a great deal and it, not surprisingly, wants to renew its annual institutional subscription. SAGE also produces the social work journal *Affilia*, which is less widely read and cited than *RSWP*, and the library is inclined to drop its institutional subscription to *Affilia*. The wise marketers at SAGE will opt to "bundle" together a large collection (some in high demand, others less so) of social work and behavioral science journals and offer an electronic subscription for the whole collection at a price dramatically lower than the cost of individually subscribing to all the journals in the bundle. Libraries have tended to snap up this offer, with two effects. Gradually, the proportion of libraries offering solely hard-copy access to journals in their periodicals collection is dropping relative to that of those offering online access to a larger-than-they-could-otherwise-afford collection of journals. Again, the result is that, while hard-copy subscriptions are remaining stable, online subscriptions are dramatically increasing due to the financial incentives involved in bundling. Thus, low-cost (to the publishers), Web-based subscription access to journals is directly subsidizing the continuing existence of the more expensive hard-copy versions of journals. The number of institutional libraries subscribing to *RSWP* hovered around 400 for many years, but since the implementation of electronic bundling that number has more than doubled; over 900 libraries now subscribe to the journal, and they usually provide faculty and students with the capacity to download articles for free. For example, in 2006, over 74,000 copies of articles that were published in *RSWP* were downloaded (most for free, via university subscriptions, but some via pay-per-view) by scholars. These Web-based developments have really facilitated the ability of scholars to access social work research—and this is a good thing for all journals.

There has yet to appear a well-known social work journal that began and is maintained exclusively online. But most of the social work journals that originated in hard-copy version are transitioning to concurrent publication of hard-copy and online versions, and this is generally a positive development. I recently had an article (Thyer, 2007) published in the *Clinical Social Work Journal.* The online version was available in November 2006, while the hard-copy journal did not appear in print until February 2007. The PDF version was made widely available to subscribers through the journal's Web site several months in advance of the print publication, and freely to folks affiliated with my university (which has an institutional library subscription). Individual articles are also available for purchase on a pay-per-download basis to social workers who do not subscribe to the journal or who lack library access but wish to obtain a copy of this particular article.

We may well see the eventual demise of the print journal, but we are a long way from it. For now, publishing in traditional hard-copy journals (that support concurrent online versions) remains the first-choice option for social work scholars. I will have some more to say about the pros and cons of publishing in exclusively online journals in Chapter 2.

Journals Lend Themselves to the Correction of Errors

An article appearing in a journal will be read by many persons, not a few of whom will be carefully scrutinizing it for mistakes, errors of omission such as failing to cite some seminal prior research, or errors of commission such as applying the incorrect method of statistical analysis or of misinterpreting data. And sometimes, after publication, the original author will realize that he or she made a mistake! Most journals recognize these realities and provide venues for corrections. Minimally it can take the form of the author publishing, in a subsequent issue of a the journal, an *erratum* notice—an acknowledgment of a mistake in the original publication along with a few corrected sentences, a reanalyzed statistical test, or a table containing corrected figures. Or a reader, Dr. X, may be motivated to write a more elaborate critique of the original piece, outlining its errors and providing presumptively corrective information, and then send this to the journal's editor with a request that it be published in the interests of scientific accuracy. If the editor accepts such a response, he or she will usually invite the authors of the offending piece to prepare a rebuttal defending their original work or (rarely) a grateful response acknowledging that they did indeed make a mistake and are ever so pleased that their mistake has been graciously corrected by Dr. X. In this way research errors can be corrected promptly, rather than exist uncorrected for decades. This self-corrective potential exists to a far lesser degree with other forms of scholarship such as a book chapter or a conference paper, and it represents another advantage of journal articles over other types of research contributions.

Summary

Publishing journal articles has been and likely will remain for the foreseeable future the most prestigious and productive means of disseminating the results of social work research. Journal articles reach more readers more rapidly than most other ways of communicating research information, and the process of blind peer review used to select manuscripts for publication is believed to be a screening mechanism that produces articles of higher quality than other ways of choosing what research articles to publish. Accordingly, publishing journal articles is the more valuable currency (at least in the social work academic community) relative to presenting papers at conferences, posting research papers on blogs or personal Web sites, or reporting original research in books or book chapters. This "pecking order" has been in place for decades, and the contingencies that gave rise to it remain operative. Thus, the relative status of journal articles as the "leaders of the pack" is unlikely to change in the near future.

2

Targeting One or More Potential Journals

Before you engage in writing your research article you should consider the specific journal, or at least the general type of journal, you plan to submit your work to. Some journals may be very familiar to you. If you belong to the National Association of Social Workers you receive *Social Work*; if you belong to the Council on Social Work Education you get the *Journal of Social Work Education*; if you belong to the Society for Social Work and Research you probably get *Research on Social Work Practice*. But these are the tip of the iceberg. Just how many English-language social work journals are there? You might be surprised to learn that one recent tabulation located over 70 such professional journals (Thyer, 2005), so you may have many more potential outlets for your research article than you initially thought. This listing of the names of English-language social work journals appears in Box 2.1, and a Google search can usually help you locate a given journal. Another really good resource is a Web-based document titled *Journals in Social Work and Related Disciplines*, compiled by Professors Patrick Leung and Monit Cheung, who are affiliated with the Graduate College of Social Work at the University of Houston (Leung & Cheung, 2007). This document is updated periodically (most recently in February 2007) and is available for free on the Web at http://www/sw/uh.edu/communityoutreach.

cwep_title_IVE.php. As current and helpful as it is, however, it possesses its own peculiarities. It does list most of the journals (but not all) appearing in Box 2.1, along with the contact information for the editor and the Web site (if any) of each, and it notes whether or not the journal uses an online submission portal. However, its listing of journals in related disciplines appears very haphazard. Very few journals in the fields of behavior analysis and therapy, psychiatry, or clinical psychology are listed, for example, so I view it as most helpful as a resource for contact information about social work journals, not as a comprehensive listing about journals in related fields.

Because journals usually have some sort of focus or a specific type of article they are aimed at publishing, you should become generally familiar with those journals that tend to publish research similar to that which you have in hand or anticipate writing up. Although most social work journals require writers to format their articles in APA style, some use a modified APA style, and a few use an entirely different style, so if you have a particular journal in mind, at the very least find out for sure what writing style it requires and prepare your manuscript accordingly. But it is not that simple: there is a wide array of important considerations to take into account when selecting a journal to submit your manuscript to. Box 2.2 provides a list of general guidelines for selecting a journal, and here are a few questions to ask yourself in this regard.

Should I Submit My Research Manuscript to a Social Work Journal or to a Non–Social Work Journal?

This is a fundamental issue that you should face up front, as there are pros and cons to each choice, as well as the local departmental norms to consider. Articles published in a social work journal are more likely to be read by other social workers, whereas articles appearing in journals affiliated with other disciplines (e.g., psychology, sociology, education, public health, medicine, psychiatry) are more likely to be read by members of those disciplines. There are also many interdisciplinary fields such as child welfare, domestic violence, addiction, mental health,

Box 2.1. English-Language Social Work Journals

Journals Published by Haworth Press (www.haworthpress.com)

> *Administration in Social Work*
> *Journal of Ethnic and Cultural Diversity in Social Work*
> *Journal of Evidence-Based Social Work*
> *Journal of Family Social Work*
> *Journal of Forensic Social Work*
> *Journal of Gay and Lesbian Social Services*
> *Journal of Gerontological Social Work*
> *Journal of HIV/AIDS & Social Services*
> *Journal of Human Behavior in the Social Environment*
> *Journal of Policy Practice*
> *Journal of Progressive Human Services*
> *Journal of Psychosocial Oncology*
> *Journal of Religion and Spirituality in Social Work*
> *Journal of Social Service Research*
> *Journal of Social Work in Disability & Rehabilitation*
> *Journal of Social Work in End-of-Life & Palliative Care*
> *Journal of Social Work in Health Care*
> *Journal of Social Work in Long Term Care*
> *Journal of Social Work in Mental Health*
> *Journal of Social Work Practice in the Addictions*
> *Journal of Spirituality and Religion in Social Work*
> *Journal of Teaching in Social Work*
> *Psychoanalytic Social Work*
> *Smith College Studies in Social Work*
> *Social Work with Groups*
> *Social Work in Health Care*
> *Social Work in Mental Health*
> *Social Work in Public Health*

Journals Published by the National Association of Social Workers

> *Children in Schools*
> *Health and Social Work*
> *Social Work*
> *Social Work Abstracts*
> *Social Work Research*

(continued)

Box 2.1. (*continued*)

Social Work Journals Published by SAGE Publications (www.sagepub.com)

Affilia: The Journal of Women in Social Work
Journal of European Social Policy
International Social Work
Qualitative Social Work
Research on Social Work Practice

Social Work Journals Produced by Other Publishers

Advances in Social Work
Arete
Asia Pacific Journal of Social Work and Development
Australian Social Work
Black Caucus
British Journal of Social Work
Canadian Social Work Review
Caribbean Journal of Social Work
Child and Adolescent Social Work Journal
Child and Family Social Work
Clinical Social Work Journal
Ethics and Social Welfare
European Journal of Social Work
Families in Society
Hong Kong Journal of Social Work
Indian Journal of Social Work
International Journal of Social Welfare
Japanese Journal of Social Services
Journal of Baccalaureate Social Work
Journal of Comparative Social Welfare
Journal of Social Work
Journal of Social Work Education
Journal of Social Work Practice
Journal of Social Work Values and Ethics
Journal of Sociology and Social Welfare
Perspectives on Social Work
Practice
Professional Development
Reflections: Narratives of Professional Helping
Rural Social Work
School Social Work Journal
Social Development Issues

(*continued*)

Box 2.1. (*continued*)

Social Service Review
Social Work and Christianity
Social Work Education
Social Work Perspectives
Social Work Review
Social Work and Social Sciences Review
The New Social Worker
The Social Worker/Le Travailleur Social

A social work journal is defined here as one that contains the words *social work* or *social welfare* in the title, that is published by a school of social work, or whose editorial policy statement clearly identifies it as a disciplinary social work journal. This admittedly restrictive definition excludes many journals that social workers may edit or publish in that describe themselves as "interdisciplinary" or that relate to a field of practice to which many disciplines contribute (e.g., child welfare, public policy, human services).

and so forth, all of which support many different interdisciplinary journals. A really great article on preventing child abuse and neglect appearing in a child abuse and neglect journal will be read by more specialists (from many disciplines) with a focus on child abuse and neglect, and such an article will have a greater impact in the child abuse and neglect field if it is published in such a journal relative to appearing in a disciplinary social work journal. It is also a sad but true observation that articles appearing in social work journals are less likely to be cited by other authors in subsequent years relative to articles published in non–social work journals.

In recognition of this fact, many authors of social work research deliberately choose to publish in non–social work journals, and it is estimated that almost half of social work articles appear in journals with a focus outside of the discipline (see Green, Baskin, & Bellin, 2002). This may be good for science in general, but it causes some intellectual impoverishment in the field of social work, as its members will be less likely to encounter useful research published afield.

According to Seipel's (2003) analysis, though, articles appearing in journals of non–social work but related fields (e.g., sociology, economics, psychology) were of marginally *less* value in obtaining tenure than works appearing in social work journals. But the effect was small and probably not worth ruminating about. Your choice should also depend on where you wish to acquire a reputation—as a social work researcher and academic or as an expert in an interdisciplinary field of practice whose professional affiliation is not as important as the quality of the research you produce. Some authors simply opt to aim for the best journal in a given field of practice (e.g., child welfare, oncology, psychotherapy, policy practice) and ignore the issue of the journal's disciplinary affiliation. This is perhaps the approach most consistent with good science. I know of some very prominent social work researchers who, disgusted with their personal experiences in submitting to social work journals, deliberately avoid trying to publish in them—a personal boycott, if you will. But be warned: if you work with a bunch of curmudgeonly senior scholars who will be voting on your tenure, and they routinely dismiss articles appearing outside the sphere of social work as unimportant, you may pay a price for your high moral position.

Should I Submit My Research Article to a High-Status Journal or a Lower-Ranked One?

There is no formal, regularly applied ranking system of any credibility in place to help us appraise the existing stable of social work journals. Which ones should be rated in the so-called top tier, middle tier, or bottom tier is clearly a matter of some subjective opinion. Sellers, Smith, Mathiesen, and Perry (2006) reported on one national survey of social work faculty in which professionals were asked to rate the overall journal quality of several dozen journals in the field. These authors did produce a ranking system derived from respondents' subjective ratings of journal quality and ended up labeling some journals as first, second, third, and lowest quartile. However, some non–social work journals were included in their analysis (e.g., *Journal of Community Psychology*, *American Journal of Community Psychology*), which compromises their results to some extent. Discretion prevents me from listing the rankings of these journals here, but the information is readily available to you in the article itself.

The more prestigious journals are likely to have a higher rejection rate, making it less likely that your work will be accepted. If your work is rejected by a top-tier journal, then you may have wasted those months awaiting the editor's decision only to find that you need to submit your paper to another journal and start the submission cycle again. This can be maddening. Submitting your work to a journal of lesser stature may mean a better chance of ultimate acceptance, but it also means an enhanced likelihood of a poorer-quality editorial review process and perhaps a longer time to wait from your article's initial acceptance until its appearance in print. Seipel (2003) had this to say on the matter: "A few outstanding projects printed in first-tier journals may be more valuable than several produced with less-respected outlets" (p. 84). This is good advice, *if* you can afford the time. If your sleep is haunted by the tick-tock of the tenure clock, and if your local department really does not discriminate in its tenure decisions between works appearing in high-versus low-quality outlets, then holding out for placement in only the highest-ranked journals may be injurious to your career in the short run.

Something to avoid is publishing your work in journals that charge a fee, sometimes disguised as a mandatory charge to purchase 100 or so reprints of your work. These journals are known as subsidy press journals or vanity outlets. There is at least one journal that tells you upon acceptance that it will be some years before your article will appear in print, but you are given the option of paying a "contribution" of $18 per printed page, and if you do so your work will be published within one year. This is strong inducement indeed to pay the early publication fee. Another requirement is the aforementioned purchase of 100 reprints, the cost of which varies according to a graduated scale based on the page length of your manuscript. A 4-page article may cost $35 for 100 reprints, a 25-page article costs $89, etc.

Now, superficially, having an article that has been published in a subsidy journal appear on your curriculum vitae may impress the uninformed, but God help you if an astute scholar is on your P & T committee and recognizes the less than stellar merits of the outlet in question. He or she will know that these are the publication outlets of last resort in the social and behavioral sciences and perhaps will damn your application accordingly. I have seen this happen. I will also admit to having published in some of these subsidy outlets myself, usually projects of marginal significance or perhaps co-authored with graduate students whose work I did not want to go to waste by remaining unpublished. There may come a time, after you have been faced with a series of rejection letters from more credible outlets, that you consciously decide to throw caution to the wind and place your work with a subsidy press, rather than have your manuscript molder in your file drawer (or hard drive), getting staler and staler. But these journals should be your option of last resort and must be resorted to sparingly, if at all. They should not form the centerpiece of your P & T binder, nor should they be the publication home of pilot studies you refer to when submitting a federal research grant proposal. It *is* a common practice for some physical and natural sciences journals to impose a page charge on authors, and this is not exceptional or pejorative, but I am not aware of any social work journal that does this. Those few among the social/behavioral sciences journals that do so are typically journals of lesser repute, in my opinion.

An emerging, legitimate business model for some journals (but not yet in social work journals, to my knowledge) is for the author of an accepted article to be given the option of paying a modest fee to have the electronic version of his or her paper placed online immediately. In either event, with the increasing availability of PDF files of articles, the need to purchase formally published reprints is minimal nowadays, and most scholars no longer put forth the time or effort to do so. If a correspondent desires a hard copy of your paper, a photocopy may suffice if he or she cannot download the article from his or her university library collection.

Should I Select a Journal Based on Its Rejection Rate?

In a word, no, because there is no reliable and independent information available on the rejection rates of social work journals. Over a decade ago, the NASW published a guide to social work journals (Marsh, 1997) outlining the name, mission, publication style, editor, rejection rate, and submission address for a limited number of social work and non–social work journals, but this was a seriously incomplete listing and was out of date by the time it appeared in print. Plus, the rejection rates given (the closest thing we've ever had to an accurate listing) were based upon the self-report of the editor of each journal, and individuals in this position may have a vested interest in inflating the numbers of manuscripts received and rejected in order to give the impression of a much busier journal and/or of higher standards than are actually the case.

Should I Publish in an Older, Established Journal or a Newer Outlet?

Both options have their merits. Established journals are more likely to have their articles picked up by the major abstracting and citation services than are newer journals or journals of generally low repute. It usually takes some years before a new journal is accepted for inclusion in these services. If a journal is not indexed and cited, then it pretty much exists only in hard copy, and this makes it very unlikely that scholars using the Internet and/or electronic databases will ever encounter (and cite) it. However, newer journals may take a shorter time to review, accept, and publish your work; in fact, they may be begging for submissions. But sometimes new journals do not survive. They may publish for a few issues, or a few years, but never really take off enough to become financially solvent. This is unpredictable, of course.

For over 20 years, the Mandel School of Applied Social Sciences, a CSWE-accredited social work program at Case Western Reserve University, sponsored and published the *Journal of Applied Social Sciences* (*JASS*). It was a respectable journal but decidedly third tier, in my opinion. Articles published in it (like some of mine were!) are now very difficult to locate. Few libraries maintain old hard-copy issues of out-of-print journals, and old *JASS* articles are not maintained on any Web site. Unless one is able to locate the author of one of these *JASS* articles and that author is willing to mail a photocopy of his or her work, it can be difficult to locate even a hard copy. The *Journal of Social Work in Long-Term Care*, previously published by Haworth Press, is another journal that has been discontinued. If you publish something in a journal that later goes out of business, the likelihood that other scholars will be able to readily access it is very low indeed. The risk of this happening is higher with a newly established journal.

How Long Does It Take for an Initial Decision to Be Made?

Once you submit your research article, keep track of the time. If the journal uses a Web-based portal to process submissions, you should get word within a day or two that the journal has received your article and that it is being processed for review; this may take a couple of weeks if the journal still requires you to submit a hard-copy manuscript (though this is increasingly rare). Sometimes the editor will make an initial determination and decide that your article is simply inappropriate for that particular journal, in which case the manuscript will be returned to you very soon, and you will be free to send it elsewhere. There are no systematic databases for you to consult on how long, on average, social work journals take to make initial editorial decisions; you must rely on colleagues to tell you of their experiences. I have conducted two survey studies (Barker & Thyer, 2005; Thyer & Myers, 2003) of published social work authors whose articles have appeared in some 20 different social work journals and reported a variety of comparative statistics regarding their experiences, including how long it took them to get a decision. But the response rates were not very high, so the representativeness of the results is unknown. However, these are the only empirical data with bearing on the topic that I am aware of.

What About Publication Lag Times?

"Lag time" is the length of time that elapses between when your article is officially accepted and when it physically appears in print. Social work journals in general have a hideously long lag time, often several years, although this varies by journal. You can unsystematically estimate lag times for those journals that publish (often at the end of an article) the dates that the work was received and finally accepted by comparing those dates with the publication date of the issue it appeared in. Obviously, the longer this lag time, the less satisfactory a potential journal outlet is. Even the best journals take about a year. This is unfortunate for a number of reasons. Those works that do appear may be rather "stale." Long lag times discourage our best researchers from submitting to social work journals at all, and they drive down the all-important impact factor of our journals.

What is a Journal's Impact Factor?

What is an impact factor (IF), you may ask? It is a rather simple descriptive statistic calculated by a database called the *Web of Science* (WOS) (also known as the Journal Citation Reports), and it refers to the extent to which an article appearing in a given journal is likely to be cited anywhere in the journal literature within 2 years of the original article's appearance in print. This includes citations not just in the journal in which the article was published but in any journals published during the next 2 years. The WOS database is likely accessible through your local university library, and it contains crucial information, updated annually, on over 25 social work journals (some good and some not so good). You can turn to the WOS social work journal listings to see how the various social work journals are ranked according to this impact factor, and how these rankings change year by year. Generally speaking, the higher a journal's IF, the more likely it is that work published in that journal will be used by others, and hence the more desirable that journal is as a potential outlet for your work. If you look at the IFs for all social work journals relative to the WOS listings for journals in other fields, such as psychology, sociology, economics, etc., you can easily see that the social work journals' IFs are appreciably lower than those of most other fields. The blame for this rests with the long lag time. If you publish an article in the January 2008 issue of *Social Work* and someone else reads it and immediately cites it in a manuscript that he or she submits to *Social Work* a week later, even with a speedy editorial review process and acceptance, that journal's lag time makes it very unlikely that the other scholar's citation of your work will appear in print within the requisite 2 years needed for it to affect that journal's IF. Citations of your work after 2 years, even only 3 or 4 years after your article is published, do not affect a journal's IF. Until we can reduce our professional journals' publication lag times, our disciplinary journals' IFs (and reputations, to some extent) will be low.

You can find out the IFs of about 25 social work journals—those indexed by the WOS—by going to the WOS Web site, accessed through its home publisher, the Institute for Scientific Information. This is most easily done through your local university library system. Under their collection of databases, look for the *Web of Science* or the Journal Citation Reports, and you will be able to track down the types of information discussed in this chapter. If you have trouble finding it or gaining access, your university reference librarian should be able to help you.

Be aware, however, that IFs can be somewhat volatile, changing markedly from year to year. The reason is not necessarily that scholars are reading the journal any more or less but rather what is published each year. For example, if someone publishes a really wacky paper, a reprehensible article, or an outlandish theory, it may be rapidly picked up and cited by others a great deal—but these could be mostly negative citations wherein the article is held up to ridicule or used to illustrate poor research methodology! Although this may not be the way you'd hoped for your work to gain notice, the IF does not discriminate between positive and negative citations—it just counts them. Another factor that can artificially inflate the IF is if the editor publishes an editorial in each issue and describes and cites each article appearing in that issue. This means that each article has been immediately cited at least once—but this is not a legitimate reflection of how other scholars may be using the published work.

Another confound is the practice engaged in by some journals of publishing a major "target" article and concurrently publishing a selection of commentaries on it in the same issue, perhaps followed by an aggregated response from the author of the target article. This too can elevate a journal's IF, but is it a real reflection of how other scholars make use of research published in the journal? It is certainly questionable. One of the psychology journals with the highest IFs is *Behavioral and Brain Sciences*, and every issue is devoted to publishing one or more target articles and accompanying peer commentary and discussion. This explains its outstandingly high IF.

Is the Journal Indexed/Abstracted/Cited by the Major Services?

In the old days, your new research article was likely to be cited if an individual subscriber to the hard-copy journal it appeared in actually read and referenced it, or if a scholar physically went to the local university library to read the latest issue of the journal and perhaps made a photocopy of your article, for later perusal and possible citation. Some months later, if the journal you published in was abstracted in the hard-copy journal *Psychological Abstracts*, readers could also learn about the existence of your work via the abstract, and perhaps track it down and cite it. Nowadays, the Internet makes things considerably easier. There are many specialized databases that report the citation and abstracts of articles relevant to various fields, including social work. The Social Science Citation Index (SSCI), a part of the larger *Web of Science* database, is a major one for social work, and it is very important to ascertain whether the journal you are thinking of sending your research article to is indeed picked up by the SSCI. If it is not, nothing about your work will appear when scholars conduct an electronic literature search using the SSCI, even if they type in keywords relevant to your article or your name. It will be as if your article did not exist.

Information about what abstracting and indexing services review articles published in a given journal can usually be found on what is called the verso page of each issue of that journal, a page of technical information and instructions for authors. Here is what the verso page for *Research on Social Work Practice* stated in the January 2007 issue:

> **Abstracting and Indexing:** This journal is abstracted or indexed in Caredata ABSTRACTS, Caredata CD, Caredata INFORMATION

BULLETIN, Current Contents/Social & Behavioral Sciences, Current Index to Journals in Education, Health and Psychosocial Instrument, Human Resources Abstracts, Linguistics and Language Behavior Abstracts, Middle East: Abstract Index, Psychological Abstracts, PsycINFO, Research Alert, Sage Family Studies Abstracts, Sage Urban Studies Abstracts, Social Planning/Policy & Development Abstracts, Social Sciences Citation Index, Social Sciences Index, Social SciSearch, Social Work Abstracts, Sociological Abstracts, and Violence and Abuse Abstracts.

This is a pretty comprehensive listing, even if you are not familiar with all of them. The most important ones are the aforementioned Social Sciences Citation Index, PsycINFO, and *Psychological Abstracts*. These are the biggest, best, most comprehensive and consistent sources used by individuals conducting literature searches. Regrettably, our own discipline's major abstracting journal and database, *Social Work Abstracts*, is a very poorly maintained program. Although it makes great claims as to comprehensiveness, two recent independent analyses found large gaps in its coverage (Holden, Barker, Covert-Vail, Rosenberg, & Cohen, in press; Shek, in press), suggesting that social work scholars cannot rely on *Social Work Abstracts* to provide comprehensive coverage of all the journals it claims to survey. Thus, any review of the literature using this database will likely be seriously compromised. If you simply make sure that your prospective journal is picked up by SSCI and PsycINFO, you should be in fine shape insofar as other scholars being able to access your work.

Does the Journal Publish Very Many Research Articles?

Interestingly, most articles published in social work journals do not report the results of empirical research (Rosen, Proctor, & Staudt, 1999), and many of our journals emphasize nonresearch articles such as opinion pieces, essays, political exhortations, clinical and other forms of practice articles, comments on current professional issues, novel practice and education techniques, and so forth. Pick up any recent issue of the NASW's flagship journal *Social Work* and you will find a lot of non-research-based content. This is understandable to some extent, since most members of NASW are not researchers themselves and many have little interest in reading research. A very important research study, meticulously reported and crammed with statistical details, may be a truly groundbreaking piece of science yet may not fare well if reviewed by *Social Work*. Other journals, of course, specialize in publishing social work research, such as the NASW's specialty journal, *Social Work Research*; the University of Chicago's *Social Service Review* (arguably the most prestigious of the social work research journals); *Research on Social Work Practice*, produced by SAGE Publications; and Haworth Press's *Journal of Social Service Research*. Your true research article may be better suited to one of these outlets rather than *Social Work*.

But the actual numbers of research articles published each year is also important. *Research on Social Work Practice* appears bimonthly (six times a year). In 2005 this journal published 46 research articles, plus assorted essays and book reviews. *Social Work Research, Social Service Review*, and the *Journal of Social Service Research*, all produced every three months, published about 17, 24, and 33 research articles that same year, respectively. So if you are aiming for the journal that publishes the most research in social work, *Research on Social Work Practice* will look preferable, publishing over three times as many research articles as other social work research journals. But *Social Service Review* is widely seen as publishing more "solid" research articles.

Among the journals that publish research-based papers, there are those that focus on highly specific forms of research. *Research on Social Work Practice*, as an extreme example, accepts for review only three types of articles: (1) empirical outcome studies on social work practice, (2) reports on the development and testing of assessment measures useful for social work research or practice, and (3) review articles on the evidentiary foundations of a particular psychosocial treatment or of effective ways of helping clients with a particular psychosocial problem. The journal's editorial policy (reprinted in each issue) specifically states that it does not publish surveys; program descriptions; theoretical, philosophical, or conceptual works; correlational investigations; retrospective predictor studies; purely methodological articles; descriptive studies; or needs assessments. This is a *highly* restrictive policy and excludes many—perhaps the majority—of research articles produced by social work scholars. If you have authored a needs assessment, do not waste your time sending it to this particular journal. Instead, locate the names of journals that have published articles similar to yours and consider one of these as a more appropriate outlet. Conversely, if you have conducted an empirical outcome study, even a one-time, pragmatic program evaluation of a single agency's program or a single-subject study, then *Research on Social Work Practice* may be one of the more suitable outlets.

Should I Publish in a Journal Produced Solely in Electronic Form?

No—at least not if you want your work to be widely available to other scholars. A few years ago, one college of social work began an electronic journal of social work, and it ceased production after one or two issues. Of course it was never picked up by any of the abstracting or citation services, and when its Web site evaporated, all evidence of its existence (e.g., articles) disappeared. In 2004, a new, solely online social work specialty journal appeared (the *Journal of Social Work Values and Ethics*, www.socialworker.com/jswve), but its prospects for the future remain unknown. It is abstracted by *Social Work Abstracts* and *Social Science Abstracts* but not by the other, larger services, so it is hard for scholars to encounter articles appearing in this journal. Other online journals in social work are reportedly in development. Given that almost all existing high-quality social work journals are available in both hard-copy printed versions and Web-based versions, and thus possess all the ease of access touted by the advocates of electronic publication, publishing in purely electronic social work journals is not yet a recommended practice, nor is it recommended in some other scientific fields. There are some exclusively Web-based journals in the physical and natural sciences that are of good repute, but even so, hard-copy print generally remains the preferred outlet for such scholars' research papers.

Should I Seek to Publish in Journals with Larger Print Circulations?

A few decades ago, a scholar's major way of coming into contact with newly published papers was to read hard-copy journals. Back then, having a large number of print subscribers was important for a journal's impact. Nowadays we are increasingly becoming aware of new articles through accessing electronic/Web-based abstracting and indexing services, not from personal subscriptions to journals or even by perusing our university library's latest print issues. Thus, circulation figures are not as significant as in the past. The NASW's flagship journal *Social Work* is received by over 120,000 members, while the University of Chicago's journal *Social Service Review* is received by fewer than 3,000 subscribers. Nevertheless, the latter journal is far more widely cited than the former. So circulation figures are a lesser consideration than in

Box 2.2. General Guidelines for Selecting Journals to Publish In

- Give preference to journals included in the Social Science Citation Index and related large citation and abstracting services such as Psyc-INFO.
- Avoid publishing in journals that charge a publication fee or require you to purchase hard-copy reprints.
- Preferentially seek to publish in journals that make initial editorial decisions in shorter time periods.
- Preferentially seek to publish in journals with shorter lag times from acceptance to publication.
- If you are up for promotion or tenure, find out what your colleagues value more, social work or non–social work journal articles, and target your journal outlets accordingly.
- Preferentially seek to publish in journals with higher, rather than lower, impact factors.
- Seek to publish in journals that concurrently support hard-copy and electronic versions.
- Take ethically appropriate advantage of personal relationships, theoretical or methodological preferences, or editorial biases in choosing your journal.
- Preferentially submit to journals that have a decentralized system of processing manuscripts and making decisions, ones where the editor is immediately involved in all aspects of handling your manuscript.

decades past. The availability of downloadable articles from print journals via the university library's or the journal's Web site has also changed the landscape of scholarly publishing. For example, in 2006 over 74,000 articles were downloaded from the Web site of *Research on Social Work Practice.* This is a huge readership for a journal with fewer than 3,000 subscribers and illustrates how dramatically Web-based availability has facilitated our access to articles.

Take Ethically Appropriate Advantage of Theoretical or Interpersonal Factors

Some journals have a clear theoretical bias. For example, the *Clinical Social Work Journal* has an obvious predilection for articles informed by psychodynamic theory and its variations, whereas *Affilia: The Journal of Women in Social Work* endorses a feminist perspective. Obviously, if your research article is based on a favored theory or perspective, it will likely fare better with the reviewers and editors than one that ignores these views or advances an alternative/competitive orientation. *Qualitative Social Work* might not be the best destination for your latest meta-analysis article. Although much of this is common sense, it still pays to be really familiar with journals. The *Journal of Applied Behavior Analysis* and the *Journal of Applied Behavioral Science* are dramatically different journals, and a submission to the latter would likely be rejected out of hand by the former, and vice versa. Editors routinely receive submissions that are inappropriate for their journals. In the best instance the editor quickly replies to the author, declining to review the inappropriate submission and discarding or returning the manuscripts. In the worst-case scenario, the article is sent out for review and languishes for some months prior to your getting a notice of its rejection on the grounds that it is inappropriate given the journal's mission statement and editorial policy. This wastes your time and delays the ultimate publication of your article.

Editors, too, like to see their own names in print, and if an article of yours favorably cites Editor X's relevant prior publications, X may be just ever so slightly more in favor of your work than if you devoted all of it to a thorough refutation of X's life work! I am not suggesting that you gratuitously throw in a few citations to X prior to submitting your manuscript to X's journal in the hopes that it will be more likely to be accepted. But for heaven's sake, if X has published on your topic and what he or she has written is genuinely germane to your research, know that X may be a bit miffed at your omissions. Or if Editor X is seriously at odds with Dr. Y, and you extol the virtues of Y's landmark studies in your manuscript, X may question your discernment. The permutations here are multitudinous, and you cannot possibly be aware of all the subtle factors to take advantage of or of the land mines to avoid. At best, you can be aware of the more conspicuous ones and act accordingly.

Who Processes my Manuscript?

Most disciplinary journals have an editor or editor-in-chief to whom you send your manuscript. This person sees your unblinded paper and assigns it to several (blind) reviewers, most likely people on the journal's editorial board but sometimes colleagues who the editor believes have particular expertise in reviewing a paper like yours. In due course the reviewers send the editor their appraisals and recommendations, and the editor assimilates this information, makes a decision, and informs you of it. However, social work is a bit of an oddity. Our two major professional associations, the National Association of Social Workers and the Council on Social Work Education, use a different model. The elected presidents of these two organizations get to appoint the editors of the journals these groups publish, and each organization has its own publications staff. When you send in your paper to the editor care of the NASW or the CSWE, it does not go to the editor; it goes to a staff person within the organization's publications department, an individual of undoubted gifts but who in all likelihood is neither a social worker nor an experienced author of journal articles. He or she assigns your paper to members of the journal's editorial board, using the keywords accompanying the journal and matching them with a listing of keywords supposedly describing the various editorial board members' interests and expertise. Some delays may occur between the time your paper is received and the time the staff member gets your paper into the hands of the reviewers.

Ideally, the reviewers get their reviews in, but if they do not the staff may opt, sometimes months after your paper was sent out for initial review, to send it to one or more (perhaps more responsive) additional reviewers. This, too, can take a considerable amount of time. Eventually the staffer will obtain the desired two to four reviews of your paper; then and only then does the editor receive a blinded copy of it, along with the reviews. He or she makes a decision and communicates it to the staffer, who in due course relays it to you.

This takes time, much time. This centralized mechanism associated with the journals of the NASW and the CSWE of processing manuscripts and arranging their review renders these journals unusually slow in terms of how long it takes to process papers, as compared to a decentralized system lacking an intermediary staff structure wherein the editor receives the papers directly, assigns reviewers directly, and gets the reviews back directly. For years various voices within the profession have been urging the NASW and the CSWE to adopt the decentralized model outlined in the APA manual, but thus far these organizations have remained unpersuaded. Although I have been a loyal member of both organizations for over 25 years, I cannot but reluctantly recognize that this system of theirs mitigates against efficient manuscript processing. Thus, if you are interested in a more rapid review and decision-making process for your manuscript, you may wish to send your article to journals that use the decentralized model. This can be particularly significant for social work scholars seeking a promotion or the award of tenure, for which a list of accepted or published articles is a prerequisite. Be aware that waiting until 6 months prior to your tenure vote can be a recipe for failure: you must allow sufficient time for the review/acceptance/publication process to play out.

3

Preparing the Manuscript

It cannot be emphasized strongly enough that you need to be thoroughly conversant with the publication style required by the journal you are planning to submit your research manuscript to. For most social work journals, this is the style described in the APA (2001) manual. At least once, actually read it from cover to cover. You will be amazed by what you will discover and how many questions will be answered. Learning APA style is like learning statistics: it is an essential research skill that will serve you very well. Following are a couple of questions to ask yourself regarding APA style. If you are not sure or are wrong about any of these, then you really need to brush up on the rules.

1. Do I know when I should and should not include the issue number of a journal when I am listing it in my reference list?
2. Do I know when I should use single spacing?
3. Do I know when I should use bold font?
4. Do I understand the levels of headings and subheadings used in preparing articles?
5. When should the right margin be justified?

If your journal does follow APA style, make sure it does not make any modifications to it. Some journals cannot resist asking authors to adopt some idiosyncratic stylistic variations to APA, and if yours does, then of course comply with the request.

Having established your familiarity with the journal's style guidelines, you may proceed to write your research paper for submission. By the way, the correct answer to Questions 2, 3, and 5 above is the same: *never!*

To Outline or Not to Outline?

Some researchers find it very helpful to begin drafting their paper by preparing a written outline. I know I do. Others do not, and it is a matter of personal taste and experience. Whatever works for you is fine. But if you do prepare an outline, by creating it in conformity with the APA manual's approach to formatting headings you can be sure that your final paper's use of headings will be properly arranged. Here is how the APA manual (2001, p. 113) suggests organizing levels of headings (this is a good way to structure the initial outline of your paper):

Centered Uppercase and Lowercase Heading (Level 1 heading)

Centered, Italicized, Uppercase and Lowercase Heading (Level 2 heading)

Flush Left, Italicized, Uppercase and Lowercase Side Heading (Level 3 heading)

   Indented, italicized, lowercase paragraph heading ending with a period. (Level 4 heading)

      CENTERED UPPERCASE HEADING (Level 5 heading)

It is rare that a social work research article will require you to use all five levels of headings. You should begin with Level 1 and move down, reserving the use of Level 5 for reports containing multiple experiments or studies. In many instances using just two levels will suffice, as in the following example for reporting a social work outcome study:

Method (Level 1)

Clients (Level 2)

Research Design

Outcome Measures

Intervention(s)

Results

Hypothesis 1

Hypothesis 2

[etc.]

Discussion and Applications to Practice

There will be modifications to this generic outline, which is admittedly slanted toward writing an outcome study on social work practice. There are many other valuable forms of empirical research, of course, such as an exploratory study versus a descriptive study versus an explanatory study. But the language and outline modifications are minor and can be readily adapted to the particulars of your study. Feel free to tinker with your outline until you are satisfied with it, but do not throw the baby out with the bath water: you cannot place the references in the middle of the paper, or place the results before the introduction.

Once your outline is satisfactory, you can begin with the structure of the manuscript, reporting the background, conduct, and results of your research. A sample outline for structuring a social work research study appears in Box 3.1.

Establish the Default Word Processing Elements for Your Paper

Assuming you are using a word processing system (most journals ask you to submit your manuscript as a Microsoft Word document), be sure your margins are set properly, with 1 inch at the top, bottom, right, and left being the standard setting. Use a standard type size of 12 characters per inch (CPI), with Times New Roman or Courier as the selected font. Set the line spacing for double spacing and leave it there. Use double spacing throughout the entire manuscript, including tables and the list

Box 3.1. Sample Outline for Structuring a Social Work Practice
        Research Paper

Title page
Abstract page
Introduction (conclude with one or more hypotheses, if it is an explanatory or
interventional study)
                                    Method
Clients [or Participants]
Agency Settings (this can be omitted in non-practice-related studies)
Research Design
Outcome Measures [Dependent Variables]
Social Work Intervention(s) [Independent Variables]
                                    Results
(Order your results by addressing the evidence pertaining to each hypothesis in turn)
Discussion and Applications to Practice [Discussion and Implications for Social Work]
                                  References
                            Tables, if any (one per page)
                Figure caption page (if any; all captions listed on one page)
Figures (if any; one per page)

Alternative terms for some other forms of research are in brackets.
This is an illustration for an empirical outcome study manuscript or other forms of quantitative
research. This can be modified for other methods of inquiry, such as qualitative studies.

of references. It is very common for authors to single-space their references, but this is not correct APA style. Do not do it. Set your word
processor to automatically insert a header and page number in the upper
right-hand corner of each page, beginning with the title page. If you do
not know how to do this, take the time to find out. Every page of your
paper, except pages with figures on them, should have such a header and
page number. The header should be two or three words that convey
something about your paper, as in, for example,

                                    Batterer-Intervention Program 1
The header phrase is not the same as the keywords you provide so that
your article can be indexed. Do not manually insert the header and page
number on each page. If you do, each time you edit your paper you
will likely throw off the pagination, and soon these headers and page
numbers will be scattered throughout your paper, rather than seques-

tered at the top of each page in their proper position. Do not have page numbers inserted at the bottom of each page, whether centered, right, or left.

Parts of the Manuscript

Title Page

Having set up the default properties of the entire paper, you can compose the title page, which actually has only three simple elements. Immediately underneath the header (double-spaced, of course) is something called the running head, which is just an abbreviated title. It should be flush left and in all uppercase letters. Keep it 50 characters or less, spacing and punctuation included.

Next, list the title of your paper using upper- and lowercase letters; the title should be placed in the upper half of the page, centered between the left and right margins. Do not use boldface type, and of course if the title covers more than one line it should be double-spaced. There is an art to composing a good title. It should convey what your research paper is about without excessive words. In fact, many journals ask that titles be 12 words or less in length. This is a good idea. Avoid superfluous phrases such as "A Pilot Study," "An Experimental Investigation," etc. Among those I have written for research papers, some titles that I think are fairly decent include the following:

An Empirical Evaluation of the Editorial Practices
of Social Work Journals

Academic Affiliations of Social Work Journal Authors:
A Productivity Analysis from 1994–1998

Serving the Homeless: Evaluating the Effectiveness
of Homeless Shelter Services

Evaluating the Effectiveness of Short-Term Treatment
at a University Counseling Center

Ages of Onset of DSM-III Anxiety Disorders

Discriminant and Concurrent Validity of Two Commonly
Used Measures of Test Anxiety

The title should convey what the paper is about in a pithy manner, in about 12 words or less, as mentioned, and it should avoid unneeded phrases. Sometimes you can come up with a title that describes not only what the paper is about but also what you found, as in the following examples from some of my own work:

Ethanol Retards Desensitization of Simple Phobias in Non-Alcoholics

Fear of Criticism is Not Specific to Obsessive-Compulsive Disorder

Another option is to have your title pose an attention-grabbing question:

Do the Families of Children with Developmental Disabilities
Obtain Recommended Services?

Developing Discipline-Specific Knowledge for Social Work:
Is It Possible?

Underneath the title should be the double-spaced name of the first author and his or her institutional affiliation. It will be helpful in your own career to select a professional version of your name to appear on all of your publications. Stick with this name over the years, as this will help folks to locate your publications when an electronic literature search of your articles is undertaken. I have used "Bruce A. Thyer" and avoided variations such as "B. A. Thyer," "Bruce Thyer," "B. Allen Thyer," etc. Sticking to a professional name can be especially important if you have occasion to change your name over the years. I know one highly productive woman social worker who has been married several times and has changed her legal name each time. But she has consistently used her professional name (her maiden name) over the years, and this was very smart. Also, note that, according to APA style, you do *not* list any degrees after your name. Not your PhD, your MSW, or your BA—no degrees at all. And certainly do not list a series of degrees, as in "BA, MSW, PhD"—this is decidedly *déclassé*. Also, do not list any professional credentials after your name, such as ACSW or LCSW, or your registration as a hypnotherapist or any other certification. A few journals that otherwise follow APA style do list such things, so it is always wise to consult a recent issue, but in general do not list your degrees or credentials.

Underneath your name you should include your institutional affiliation. If it is a college or university, just list that college or university. If the university has more than one campus, list the campus you are with. Do not list your school or college of social work, other departmental affiliation, or any places where you have concurrent appointments. These may appear, if at all, in the corresponding address you provide later on in the manuscript. If the affiliation is not a college or university (for instance, an agency or private firm), also include the city and state. A sample title page appears in Box 3.2.

Please notice what is *missing* from the title page: There are no footnotes thanking all the people who helped you. There is no funding source listed. There is no corresponding address or e-mail. APA style does not include these elements on the title page; they appear later in the paper and will be discussed later in this chapter.

Now, having created the perfect title page, it is time to move on to preparing and formatting the abstract page.

Abstract Page

The second page of your paper is headed with the word "Abstract," placed on the center of the first line (under the header). Do not place the title of your paper here again. Double-space (remember, this should be done automatically by your word processor because you have formatted it for double-spacing at the top of the title page), adjust your justification

Box 3.2. Sample Title Page

Batterer Intervention Programs 1

Running Head: EVALUATING A STATEWIDE BATTERER INTERVENTION
SYSTEM

Program Completion and Re-Arrest in a Batterer Intervention System

Larry W. Bennett

University of Illinois at Chicago

Charles Stoops

Dominican University

Christine Call

University of Arkansas at Little Rock

Heather Flett

Taking Back Our Lives, Chicago, Illinois

---

to the left, and begin writing your abstract. Do not indent the first line of
the abstract.

The abstract may be the most important paragraph of your whole
paper. It will likely be read far more times than the paper in its entirety,
and it will be reproduced by the various abstracting and indexing services connected with the journal in order to tell people about what you
did. Abstracts (as per APA style) are usually limited to 120 words, which
is a frustratingly brief limit when you are attempting to convey what you
did, why and how you did it, and what you found. Here is what the
abstract of an empirical research report should contain:

- the issue or problem under investigation;
- information about the participants, listing age, race, gender and
  other pertinent features;

- the research method (correlational study, a quasi-experiment, a randomized controlled trial, a multiple-baseline design, etc.), the intervention(s), and the outcome measures;
- the results, including statistical significance and effect sizes; and
- the conclusions and any applications to practice.

This list varies a bit from the illustration provided in the APA manual, given the unique aspects of social work research relative to psychological research (e.g., we do not engage in research with animals, we rarely use apparatus). Some journals now require abstracts to include three or four generic headings, such as *Objective, Method, Results,* and *Conclusion,* and the use of these really enhances the readability of the abstract. Even if the journal you are submitting to does not require their use, there is nothing to prevent you from including them if you wish. A sample abstract appears in Box 3.3, and you can see how adding some generic headings can be useful to the reader.

With the abstract all shipshape, you can move on to preparing the text itself. Please note, though, that some writers prepare the abstract after the entire article is completed, rather than at the beginning of the writing process.

Box 3.3. Sample Abstract with Headings

Objective: The authors examine the effects of batterer intervention program (BIP) completion on domestic violence re-arrest in an urban system of 30 BIPs with a common set of state standards, common program completion criteria, and centralized criminal justice supervision. **Method:** 899 men arrested for domestic violence were assessed and completed 1 of 30 BIPs. At 2.4 years after intake, the authors reviewed arrest records and modeled domestic violence re-arrest using instrumental variable estimation and logistic regression. **Results:** There were 14.3% of completers and 34.7% of non-completers re-arrested for domestic violence. Completing a BIP reduces the odds of re-arrest 39% to 61%. **Conclusions:** This study supports efforts to engage and retain men in gender-specific BIPs, as well as the value of examining larger systems of BIPs.

Keywords: battered; domestic violence; criminal justice; intervention.

Source: Bennett, Stoops, Call, & Flett (2007, p. 42).

Introduction

The third page of your manuscript begins the text itself. Place the title of your paper again at the top of the page, double-space down, indent the first paragraph, and begin to write your introduction. There are many ways to structure this. Several paragraphs describing the problem area or topic you are researching, with some of the unanswered questions you address in the paper, is always a nice way to begin. You can conceive of the introduction portion of your paper as a conceptual funnel: start out broad, addressing a general area of practice, then move to more specific topics, culminating in one or more specific hypotheses your study will test. Here is an example of what I mean:

General area: Child welfare

More specific area: Child abuse and neglect

More specific area: Family reunification

More specific area: Family preservation programs

A research question: Does the *Family Safety* program provided by the Florida Department of Children and Families promote family reunification?

A hypothesis: Children and families enrolled in the DCF *Family Safety* program in Leon County will experience a significantly higher percentage of family reunification after one year than children and families who received standard protective services.

Or,

General area: Domestic violence

More specific area: Men battering women

More specific area: Batterer intervention programs (BIPs)

A research question: Are men who complete a BIP less violent afterwards?

A hypothesis: Men who successfully complete the Leon County BIP will be re-arrested for domestic violence significantly less often during the 24 months following program completion compared to men who dropped out of the program.

Or,

General area: Chronic mental illness

More specific area: Schizophrenia

More specific area: Psychosocial treatments

More specific area: Assertive Community Treatment (ACT)

A research question: Does participation in ACT reduce re-hospitalization?

A hypothesis: Clients seen at the Leon County Outpatient Program who have enrolled in the ACT program will have lower rates of rehospitalization over 2 years than similar outpatients who do not receive ACT.

Your literature review can selectively address each of these areas with one or more paragraphs. Consider including some international, national, or state statistics on the prevalence and costs of the problem. It is important to provide convincing evidence that the issue you are researching is a socially important one and not a trivial matter solely of interest to a musty scholar in some area of social science. Then try and seamlessly transition to a review of various interventions for this problem, discussing how social workers have tried to address it. This in turn can segue into the specifics of the present study and how there is a need to evaluate local/state/national services. Depending on the nature of the issue (we do not always study "problems"), you may wish to focus on prior empirical research, prior theoretical publications, or both. If there is a lot of existing research, a good way to organize it is chronologically, reviewing the oldest published study first, then the next oldest, and so on, up to the most recent empirical work. Your review may naturally reveal some lacunae or under-researched areas in the literature. Perhaps the psychosocial intervention was developed and successfully applied by nurses but has never been tested for use by social workers, hence justifying the present study. Perhaps it is an effective treatment when applied to individual clients, but no one (to date!) has examined its efficacy when applied in groups (hence justifying your present study). Your introduction should leave the reader with a clear understanding of the issue being addressed, the context of the current study in light of prior work, and how your study attempted to augment what is known about a given treatment or issue.

It is highly recommended that you conclude your introduction with one or more specific and directional hypotheses that are clearly derived from prior empirical work or prior theory. The more specific and directional your hypotheses are, the more testable and potentially falsifiable they are, and these are characteristics of really good hypotheses. Vaguely worded hypotheses are difficult to corroborate or disprove. Lacking such sound hypotheses, your explanatory or interventional study will be seriously compromised. Hypotheses may be less central to your study if you are conducting an exploratory, descriptive, or qualitative research report. It is also a good idea to have one hypothesis for each outcome measure (dependent variable) you use in your study. Just as we recommend avoiding double-barreled questions in clinical interviews, double-barreled hypotheses—those predicting more than one relationship among variables—are to be avoided. The exception, of course, is when one is legitimately conducting a study on multivariate relationships. Crafting such hypotheses requires one to draw upon prior empirical research and theory to come up with such predictions. This is different than proposing a poorly worded, double-barreled hypothesis that is the result of sloppy thinking.

Relatedly, when designing your study, if a given measure you are assessing does not directly bear on the testing of one or more of your hypotheses, consider deleting it from your research protocol. This keeps your study from looking like a fishing expedition. Recall what a hypothesis is:

> A hypothesis predicts something that ought to be observed in the real world if a theory is correct. It is a tentative and testable statement about how changes in one thing are expected to explain changes in something else. . . . The things that hypotheses predict are called variables. . . . Most hypotheses predict which variable influences the other; in other words, which one is the cause and which one is the effect. (Rubin & Babbie, 2007, p. 49)

Although directional ("better," "worse," "less," "more") hypotheses are stronger in a scientific sense because of their greater capacity for refutation, sometimes nondirectional hypotheses (which more simply predict a change or difference among variables) are acceptable. The following are examples of good hypotheses:

> MSW students with BSWs will statistically significantly ($p<.05$) prefer using post-conventional moral reasoning, compared to MSW students with undergraduate degrees in the liberal arts, as assessed by mean scores on the Kohlberg Moral Reasoning Test.

The hypothesis predicts a difference in a particular direction and involving a statistically significant change. It mentions the groups of participants and the variables involved, and it implies a causal relationship.

> BIP Program completers will experience statistically significantly ($p<.05$) less re-arrest rates, relative to clients who prematurely terminate the BIP, two years post-BIP completion.
>
> The Pearson product-moment correlation between total GRE score and annual income of MSW applicants' family-of-origin will exceed $+.40$.

Here are some examples of poorly worded hypotheses:

> "Clients receiving psychotherapy will change."
> "The LCSW test scores of traditional versus advanced standing MSW graduates will differ."
> "Registered Republicans and registered Democrats will donate different amounts of money to charity, annually."
> "People living east of the Mississippi will not weigh the same as people living west of the Mississippi."

One problem with how these hypotheses are worded is that *any* differences or changes, occurring in *any* direction, will be supported, no matter how big or small or whether they are statistically significant or not.

A word on theory: If your research project is associated with a solid body of prior theory, then your literature review will need to analyze and summarize this literature. If your hypotheses are legitimately grounded in established theory, this should be appropriately mentioned, and later in the paper your discussion section should discuss the implications of your results for current theory. But if your project is not honestly based in established theory, it is perfectly appropriate not to include a review of relevant theory or mention of how your results build on established theory (see Thyer, 2001). Many research projects are not grounded in behavioral or social science theory, including some exploratory and descriptive studies and many evaluations of innovative programs or clinical services. These are still perfectly legitimate and potentially valuable research contributions. As noted in Rubin and Babbie (2007),

> Some valuable social work research studies, however, do not involve theory.... Other atheoretical studies might seek to describe something without attempting to explain it. (p. 48)

Method

The next major section of your research paper is where you actually describe what you did in this particular project. Begin with the Level 1 heading "Method" and then insert a Level 2 heading; in many instances this will be *Clients*. Some writers prefer the more egalitarian term *Participants*; both are acceptable. What is usually not appropriate is to use the term *Subjects*. Almost all research by social workers involves clientele, or sometimes students or other social workers. We very rarely conduct basis science inquiries that do not involve these groups, but if we do, then the more generic term *subjects* may be suitable.

Here you need to describe how you obtained your sample of clients and the time frame within which this recruitment process occurred (e.g., 1 January 2008–30 June 2008). If you attempted a true random-selection process, indicate how this was undertaken, how clients were approached, and how informed consent was obtained. If events occurred that compromised your ability to obtain a true random sample (and they almost always do, since not everyone solicited to participate will agree to do so), indicate the exact numbers approached, how many agreed or declined, the final percentage of approached individuals who agreed to participate, etc. You should also mention whether or not your study obtained institutional review board (IRB) approval. Not all social work research requires IRB oversight, but certainly most research conducted by social work academics and students using real people will need IRB review and approval (or a formal exemption). If there are legitimate reasons for why you did not seek IRB approval, state what these were, but do clearly address the issue; do not ignore it.

If you did not randomly select clients, describe how you did obtain your sample. If it was a convenience sample, where did you recruit them from, and how? If it was a snowball sampling technique, how did you locate the initial participant, and on what basis did he or she aid you in locating additional participants? The general idea here is that you wish to give the readers sufficient information as to permit them to replicate your sampling method.

Also under this method section, you may wish to add an additional subheading, *Agency Setting*, if you based your work at a particular agency and it is willing to allow you to disclose its identity. Unless there are reasons for disguising the agency's location and identity (e.g., it does not give you permission to reveal such information), go ahead and state these facts, as in, "This study was conducted at the Leon County Community Mental Health Center, located in Tallahassee, Florida." There may be legitimate reasons to disguise an agency site—the results may be embarrassing or awkward for the agency, some clients' identities may be at risk of being disclosed, or you perhaps promised management you would keep the agency's identity confidential. If such reasons don't apply, do briefly list some salient characteristics of the agency: whether it is public or private, profit or not for profit, who sponsors it, its mission or purpose, numbers of staff, clientele served, and funding sources.

Research Design

This section can usually be brief. If you used a formal and identifiable research design, identify it by name, and if it is a nomothetic design, include a schematic diagram, as can be found in research texts such as Rubin and Babbie (2007) or Royse, Thyer, Padgett, and Logan (2006). For example, a simple pretest–post-test group design is abbreviated as O_1 X O_2, whereas a pretest–post-test, no-treatment, randomized, controlled group design is diagrammed as follows:

$$R \quad O_1 \text{ X } O_2$$
$$R \qquad\quad O_1 \; O_2$$

Here, R indicates that the groups were created using random assignment, the O's represent observation or assessment periods, and X represents receipt of a treatment. Including such a diagram is often very useful to readers, especially if a complex design was used. Single-system research, of course, has its design laid out clearly in the graph or graphs used to portray data, and some approaches, such as descriptive or correlational studies, may not have formal designs at all.

Social Work Intervention

This section could also be labeled *Independent Variable*, but I prefer calling it "intervention" or "treatment" (if you are reporting an outcome study), as this is less vague; this portion of the work should address the varying treatment conditions your clients may have received. Usually one intervention, the focus of the study, is called the experimental treatment; this may be the new approach being tested. If another group of clients receives nothing, this too is a condition, called no-treatment control. Clients may also receive *treatment as usual* (TAU), or standard care, as a form of comparison; more rarely, social work clients may be assigned to receive a placebo intervention. This is not as outlandish as you may think. Over 20 years ago, LeCroy (1985) reviewed 21 outcome studies on social work practice and found that 9 actually involved assigning social work clients to a placebo control group. See also Blenkner (1962) on the use of placebo control groups in social work outcomes research.

You basically have three options available to you in describing your intervention(s). The first, and perhaps the most scientifically credible, is to describe the intervention in sufficient detail so as to permit the well-trained reader to replicate the essential or crucial elements of your practices in his or her own agency or research study. This may not be possible due to the admitted vagueness of many social work interventions or to the complexity of social care. Another constraint may be the lack of space in the research manuscript itself, particularly if the journal imposes page limitations on submissions.

A second option is to use interventions that are already widely available in protocol form; as a practice guideline, therapy algorithm, or treatment manual; and/or in the journal or book literature or elsewhere (e.g., a federal agency's Web site). In this circumstance you can describe in a couple of paragraphs what was done, then direct the reader to these existing, lengthier references, indicating that your social workers followed the protocols described therein. Such treatment manuals and practice guidelines are increasingly available for helping social work clients with a number of mental disorders, as well as for other conditions (see Howard & Jenson, 1999; LeCroy, 1994).

The third option is the least scientifically justifiable but very common when evaluating real-life social work services in agency-based settings, and that is to do the best you can in describing the interventions with full recognition that your written description is insufficient to permit others to replicate the services provided. Here there may not be even the pretense that your outcome study involved the testing of a well-proceduralized and replicable intervention. Rather, honestly and forthrightly acknowledge that this particular study involved clinical treatment as usual, or even experimental interventions, and that your description should not be viewed as a treatment protocol. Keep in mind that evaluating routine services as they are usually delivered in agencies is a worthwhile, even noble, undertaking, even if it is not the ideal scientific circumstance. Such studies can set the stage for the far more detailed analyses and investigations of apparently helpful but vaguely specified treatments, so that their critical elements can be effectively isolated in later studies in a replicable manner. By their very nature, program evaluations conducted in real-life agencies may not have very generalizable results due to the nonrepresentativeness of the clientele or the nonreproducible independent variables (treatments). Still, it is useful to know if the program's services are helpful, and such results may indeed be publishable.

Really tightly controlled outcome studies control for the integrity of the independent variable (treatment) by having treatment sessions audio- or videotaped and then having these tapes blindly evaluated by independent expert clinicians to ensure that the therapists supposedly providing treatment A are really providing their clients with treatment A, not B or some other approach. If these outside experts independently agree that A is being provided to clients assigned to condition A and B is being received by those who are supposed to receive B, then you have taken a big step toward demonstrating treatment fidelity.

Another approach is to ask the clients to rate the "credibility" or confidence they had in the treatment they received. An experimental comparison of treatment A versus treatment B is a fair test only if A and B are equivalent on factors such as believability, confidence, positive expectancies, and placebo influences that they induce in clients. Rating credibility ensures that treatments A and B differ only on the basis of the active and specific ingredients supposedly distinguishing A and B and not on differing levels of placebo-type credibility. If A is a very believable therapy and B is not, then, irrespective of the possible genuine differential effectiveness of A and B, the outcomes of A and B may differ due to their varying levels of believability. Some well-designed psychotherapy outcome studies, at the end of treatment, actually systematically assess the confidence clients had that their assigned therapy was credible. If the groups indicate equivalent levels of confidence or credibility, then these nonspecific influences can be considered controlled for as well.

This section of the manuscript is also the appropriate place to report on the characteristics of the practitioners—those who actually delivered the services provided to clients. The usual demographic bits of information go here—age, race, gender, degrees and disciplines (e.g., social work, psychology, nursing, marriage and family therapy), any specialized training they may have had in the experimental treatment, years of clinical experience, etc. It is also really a solid practice to indicate that the social workers assigned to provide services to clients in different treatment groups were indeed equivalent with respect to these demographic features and clinical experience. If it turns out that they were not, as would be the case if the social workers providing services to the experimental treatment group had many more years of practice experience than did the social workers providing services to the TAU group, then the comparison of the experimental treatment versus TAU is compromised. If this should happen and is discovered only retrospectively, it does not mean that your study is doomed. You may, for example, be able to use any differential therapist factors in an analysis of covariance, a form of analysis of variance where pretreatment differences are statistically controlled for, when examining post-treatment outcomes between groups. But keep in mind that the retrospective statistical control of experimental confounds is a poor substitute for the prospective control of such factors by means of adequate design features. By checking these things out before treatment begins, you may be able to fix them in reality before the fact (e.g., reassign more experienced social workers so this factor is equated between groups) rather than statistically after the treatments are concluded.

Outcome Measures

This section can also be called "Dependent Variables," but I think "Outcome Measures" is more informative, particularly when you are reporting an outcome study. Obviously you should list all the outcome measures you used in your research. Ideally, these will be previously published measures with well-established reliability and validity. You can refer to these by name (e.g., the Beck Depression Inventory, the Brief Psychiatric Rating Scale) and provide one or two references to prior publications that document more extensively the instrument's psychometric properties. *Measures for Clinical Practice and Research: A Sourcebook* (Fischer & Corcoran, 2007) is often used in this regard by social work researchers, but this is a secondary source, and it is a better practice to refer the reader to more primary citations in the form of journal articles, books chapters, or books. Some measures are in the public domain and available via government documents or Web sites.

Even if your outcome measure does have established reliability and validity, it will often be the case that these properties were established using normative or client samples of people who were different from those in your study. This is especially problematic when a measure was normed using Caucasian people and you have applied it in your study with minorities, or if it was originally developed in English and your clients were not native speakers of English. If such differences exist in your study, indicate them in a cautionary note to the reader.

Less well-known but previously published and validated measures may require fuller description and citations referring readers to primary publications. It is not usually necessary that you go on at great length (like you may have done in your dissertation), in effect providing a comprehensive literature review of everything ever written about the outcome measure under discussion. Your goal is to provide the reader with enough information to persuade him or her that the measure is a reliable and valid one, and that it is an appropriate choice to assess the construct(s) you are investigating in your report.

Problems can emerge if, for the purposes of your study, you invented your own outcome measure. Avoid this practice if at all possible. Most constructs you wish to assess as outcome measures will have some prior instrumentation already developed and published, and it is very likely that suitable measures will be available. Prior to inventing your own measure, be sure you have comprehensively searched the relevant literature and have ascertained that nothing appropriate already exists. It is the sign of an inexperienced researcher to create a new assessment instrument, and perhaps to even go on to run preliminary analyses on its reliability and validity, when existing measures are already available for use. The blind reviewers of your manuscript will take keen delight in pointing this out to you in their commentary, to your chagrin.

New measures cannot simply be invented and used in a social work research study that has any pretensions to credibility unless the new measure can be shown to be valid. It is exceedingly difficult to do both of these things—design and validate an outcome measure, and design and conduct a separate research project using this measure—at the same time. It is a preferred practice, if you really need to create a new measure, to do so and write up a separate report on its reliability and validity, and submit this for publication as a separate paper. Then, design and write up the separate research project that makes use of this outcome measure and refer to this other validation study, even as an article in press or under review. Springer, Abell, and Hudson (2002) and Springer, Abell, and Nugent (2002) are good resources for social workers interested in developing measurement instruments, and such an undertaking is often equivalent to conducting a dissertation study in its own right.

Results

Begin this section by describing the salient characteristics of the clients who actually participated in the study. If they were assigned to different conditions, or if such conditions occurred naturally (e.g., clients who received immediate treatment versus those who were on a waitlist for a certain time period; clients who got individual treatment versus group therapy; clients who received services from MSWs versus BSWs), describe the characteristics of each group separately. If you do this, there is no need to describe the features of all the clients in the aggregate. At a minimum, include client demographic factors such as age, race, gender, ethnic background, and socioeconomic status, if available. Be reasonable: you do not need to report tangential variables (e.g., clients' astrological signs). Report categorical and ordinal data in terms of frequencies and percentages, and report ratio and interval data in terms of N's, means, and standard deviations. Never report a mean without its associated N and SD, or a percentage without the corresponding N.

Next, it is a good practice to restate your first hypothesis (mentioned at the end of the introduction) and then report on the data that directly address the corroboration or refutation of this particular hypothesis. If you tested this hypothesis with more than one outcome measure, report the results for the first outcome measure in their entirety, then the results for the second outcome measure, and so on. Conclude with as clear a statement as is justified by your data regarding the support (or lack thereof) of this first hypothesis. Repeat this method of reporting for your second hypothesis, then your third, and so on. Be modest in your claims. At best, if the results turn out as your hypothesis predicted, you can claim that the theory (if any) the hypothesis was derived from was *supported* or *corroborated*. Only very rarely it is appropriate to claim that a theory has been proven to be true or has been validated. Conversely, if the hypothesized results do not emerge, you can claim that the theory was weakened or falsified. Curiously, scientific research is better at asserting that a theory is false than determining it is true or verified. Falsifying results obtained from a well-designed study can be truly damaging to a theory, whereas confirmatory ones at best support not only the theory the research may have been based on but also all the other theories that may have predicted the same thing. It is very rare that a given result of a social work research study can be said to have been predicted by Theory A alone, and not concurrently by Theory B, C, D, etc.

Whenever you report the results of statistically significant differences obtained using an inferential test, in addition to the name of the test (e.g., t, F, χ^2), the test's degrees of freedom, the actual test coefficient, and the actual alpha level (e.g., $p = .04$, rather than $p < .05$), you should always report some measure of effect size or proportion of variance explained (PVE) or potentially accounted for by the independent variable (treatment?). General guidance for doing this is contained in the APA manual (APA, 2001, pp. 25–26), and more specialized instructions can be found in Hudson, Thyer, and Stocks (1985), Snyder and Lawson (1993), and Thompson (1999). Basically, traditional inferential tests, such as t-tests or ANOVAs, tell us only if a difference between two variables can be reliably attributed to chance or not. They do not say much about the size or importance of any reliable difference; this is what an effect size or reporting the PVE does. An effect size estimate is easy to calculate if sufficient information is reported relating to the inferential tests. This is one reason that we need to include N's and SDs with every mean reported, and N's each time we report a percentage.

When we do so, it discloses effects that are statistically reliable (e.g., not very likely due to chance) but that exert only a trivial influence on outcome measures. This added transparency promotes a form of statistical conservatism and tempers our natural tendency to make exaggerated claims based solely on traditional levels of statistical significance.

Another conservative (and hence desirable) practice is to report the results of prospective power analyses conducted prior to undertaking your study. These can be used to justify your sample size(s). If you did not obtain expected statistically significant differences, a retrospective power analysis at this stage in the results section can inform the reader of the likely sample size that would have been necessary to achieve statistical significance. To be honest, though, social work researchers' ability to enhance their sample sizes is far more limited than that of, say, psychologists who do research with undergraduate students. Our research usually is based on agency-based client samples of convenience, over which we have limited influence: we simply can't conjure up more abused children, rape victims, or clients with severe mental illness in order to ensure that our studies have sufficient statistical power.

It is parsimonious to include in your results section only those data that bear on your specific hypotheses. Sometimes it is tempting to include all the many interesting and unexpected findings you obtained, even if they have little or no bearing on your hypotheses. I recommend that you avoid this practice. Remember that the likelihood of finding statistically significant results increases as you perform multiple tests or correlations. If you begin looking at many correlations among variables, or at multiple within- or between-group differences using many separate t-tests or χ^2 analyses, it would be surprising *not* to have unexpected and interesting findings emerge on the basis of chance alone. For example, if you use $p < .05$ as your alpha level and you run 100 tests (not hard to do if you have 10 or 11 variables to correlate with one another), probability theory would predict that you'd get five statistically significant correlations, just due to chance alone! Run 20 t-tests, and don't get all excited if one pops up as significant: with $p < .05$, chance predicts that 1 out of 20 such tests run will be significant. Also, the larger the sample size in your study, the more likely it is that any minor differences you find will indeed be "statistically significant." But do not confuse finding a reliable difference (significant in the statistical sense of the term) with finding an important one (significant in the usual sense of the term).

If you do run multiple tests, then the alpha level should be adjusted to take into account the number of tests run. One common way to do this is to use Bonferroni's inequality, also known as Dunn's multiple comparison test. Simply take your usual critical alpha level, say .05, and divide it by the number of tests you plan to run. So, if you plan to run two t-tests, instead of the usual one the t-tables are based upon, then the real, adjusted alpha level you should conservatively use is .05/2, or .025. In other words, using the Bonferroni correction makes it harder to claim that you obtained a statistically significant difference. If you plan to run 10 tests, then the Bonferroni adjustment is .05/10, or .005. Instead of declaring a significant finding if $p<.05$, it would have to reach $p<.005$—a much more stringent standard! You can see how this results in a more conservative approach to statistical significance testing, but adherence to the principles of reporting effect sizes, combined with the practice of adjusting your alpha level according to the number of tests actually performed, will result in more credible scientific findings. We will end up learning about fewer effects or differences, perhaps, but the ones that survive this level of statistical scrutiny will be really powerful, robust effects. And in applied or field research involving real clients with real problems, some of which are life threatening, we need to adopt higher standards of scientific rigor and not be content with the lower standards associated with less practical fields of inquiry.

Also, examine your serendipitous outcomes or relationships—not those associated with your prospectively laid-out statistical tests but those curious little gemstones of findings unexpectedly gleaned from your reams of data. Treasure them, keep them, hug them closely to your breast—but do not bother reporting them in your research study. Rather, use them as the jumping-off place from which to conduct a fresh prospective study to see if the unexpected findings can be replicated. Then prepare an independent article with your original findings and contexts along with your replicated result. This will help ensure that your unexpected finding, by being prospectively replicated, is a genuine phenomenon and not an artifact of multiple statistical analyses. This is also a good way for theory to be developed or expanded based upon unexpected findings. When reporting the results of your original study, strive very hard to limit yourself to a bald recitation of the evidence directly relevant to your explicitly stated prospective hypotheses.

Discussion

This last section can be headed simply "Discussion," but some journals provide other instructions. *Research on Social Work Practice*, for example, requires it to be labeled "Discussion and Applications to Practice" and further asks authors to be sure to really discuss actual applications to practice of the findings, not merely possible implications. For this particular journal, with its focus on practice research, such an applied emphasis is highly desirable.

First, the discussion section should summarize the results and state whether or not the pattern of hypotheses was corroborated or disconfirmed. If your results can be accounted for by some rival hypothesis or hypotheses, it is a sign of intellectual integrity to recount such possibilities here, along with why you believe them to be either legitimate alternative explanations or not very viable. You should also include, if appropriate, an analysis of how these results may be integrated with prior theory. But for heaven's sake, do not toss in any gratuitous references to a theory unless your study was really based on it. Such *post hoc* or retrospective theorizing reverses the directionality of the theory–research relationship.

The discussion should also include a dispassionate review of the limitations of your study. Some of these may have occurred to you only after the study was completed, as in finding out that the supposedly independent assessors has discussed their ratings with each other during the study, that the treatments had major differences in terms of credibility as perceived by the clients, or that one of the therapists mixed up the treatments he or she was providing. Low interrater agreement on observational data can compromise findings, as can excessive or differential client dropout between treatment conditions. These are all retrospectively realized limitations, but there may be some problems with your study that you were aware of from the onset. For example, you may have known from the beginning that you could recruit only a small number of clients, and that this would affect the ultimate statistical power of your study. In a pilot or preliminary study this may be acceptable. Maria Spinelli (1997), for example, had only 13 clients in the study that led to her initial three-page description of application of interpersonal psychotherapy for depressed antepartum women, a relatively low number resulting in low statistical power. However, the preliminary but positive results she obtained justified the expense of time and resources required to do a larger, randomized, controlled trial a few years later (Spinelli & Endicott, 2003). Interpersonal psychotherapy was invented by a social worker, so studies like these are of particular interest to our field.

The lesson here is that flaws need not be damning. No one has conducted the perfect study, and by bringing possible problems and confounds to the attention of readers, you let them know that you are not oblivious to these issues and have carefully considered them in arriving at your conclusions. You will be more respected by informed reviewers and readers for having done this; if you do not mention problems, it may appear that you are pretending they do not exist or hoping they will not occur to the reader.

Another good thing to bring attention to in the discussion is suggestions for future research. How could someone creatively build upon what you have done to design a better study, a more solid investigation of a social work intervention, or a more rigorous test of some psychosocial theory? Move beyond superficial recommendations (e.g., a larger sample of clients, a more diverse group of participants) to meatier suggestions, such as the following:

- Employ the principle of triangulation in future assessments of client functioning before and after treatment, involving client self-report *and* the views of spouses, caregivers, parents or teachers.
- Include direct observations of behavior in real-world contexts, with appropriate tests of interrater agreement.

• Move beyond assessment of presenting problems to more encom-
passing dependent variables, such as quality of life, global assessment of functioning, or life satisfaction.

Try to suggest ideas that will really advance the research agenda and
not just result in a meagerly different replication study that would in-
crease knowledge a teeny little bit. Help folks avoid some of the mistakes
you made or anticipate some difficulties you failed to foresee. These are
the kinds of meaningful suggestions that are really worth including in a
discussion section.

Once you have completed the discussion section of your research
paper, you can give yourself a bit of a pat on the back: you are almost
finished. On to the references!

References

This section of your paper, unlike the last few, should begin on a new
page, with the Level 1 heading of "References" appearing centered on
the first line below the header. Make sure your word processor has the
spacing set at 2 (double-spaced), as it was for the prior portions of the
manuscript. You must be confident that you know how to format references according to APA style. It is complicated at first, but it actually
makes a great deal of sense once you get the hang of it.

First of all, the references are alphabetized according to the last name
of the first author, and the first line of each separate reference is flush
with the left margin, while the remaining lines for that reference are
indented. The second reference's first line is again set flush left, with the
remaining lines indented. See the examples below:

Holosko, M. J. (2006). A suggested author's checklist for submitting
manuscripts to *Research on Social Work Practice*. *Research on
Social Work Practice, 16,* 449–454.
Holosko, M. J. (2006). A suggested author's checklist for submitting
manuscripts to *Research on Social Work Practice*. *Research on
Social Work Practice, 16*(4), 449–454.

I included two versions of the citation for Dr. Holosko's article to illustrate one very common mistake made by authors when citing journal articles. Can you tell which version is the correct one? Do you even see the difference? The common mistake, illustrated in one of the examples above, is for authors to include the issue number in a reference when it should not be there, or to omit it when it should be included. The default rule is that it is almost always correct *not* to include the issue number. What is all this about? Well, most journals can be referenced by the year of publication, the volume number, and the issue number. The issue number refers to the first, second, third, etc. issue produced within each volume. Now, most journals are paginated by year, meaning that if issue #1 contains pages 1 through 120, then issue #2 begins with page 121, and so on. So by the end of the year, the articles may be on pages 400 to 700 of that volume and the journal may be on the fourth, fifth, or sixth issue. The APA guideline is simple: *do not* include the issue number for journals paginated by year, but *do* include the issue number for journals paginated by issue (there are very few of them). *Research on Social Work Practice*, for example, is paginated by year and releases six issues per volume, with one volume per year. Mike Holosko's article, cited above, appeared in the July 2006 issue of *RSWP*, in the 4th issue. Which version is consistent with APA style? The first one, because it *omits* the issue number.

How do you know if a journal is paginated by year or by issue? There are at least three ways to tell. Look at your reference; if it begins in the 200-page range or higher, you can be almost certain the journal is paginated by year (few journals offer more than 150 pages per issue), and you should omit the issue number. The second way to tell is to obtain a copy of the journal in question. If issues 2, 3, or 4 begin with page 1, then it is paginated by issue, and you should include the issue number when formatting your reference. If you have only the first issue of a volume at hand, you will not be able to tell. The third way is to contact the editor and ask! I admit that this level of formatting minutia is excruciatingly tedious, but as the architect Mies van der Rohe said, "God is in the details."

Another APA style guideline that is often overlooked is to include page numbers when citing chapters. Other than these two points, I do not intend to take you through all the arcane lore pertaining to the citing of references that can be found in the APA style manual. As mentioned earlier in this book, you should read the style manual yourself from cover to cover and learn it well.

Author Note

After you complete your reference section, begin a new page and title it, centered on the first line under the header,

Author Note

Here is where you include information about the authors that the journal may ask for, any acknowledgments or thanks, your funding source, any conflicts of interest, and the postal and e-mail addresses for the corresponding author. You may list your terminal degree here with your corresponding address. Again, it is not a recommended practice to list multiple degrees, credentials, or affiliations. Box 3.4 contains a sample author note. You will see that it, too, contains a header and consecutive page number.

Tables

After the Author Note page come the article's tables, if any. Each table goes on its own page. Do not place two or more tables on one page. Use

Box 3.4. A Sample but Fictitious Author Note Page

Qualitative Significance 23

Author Note

Bruce A. Thyer is a Professor of Social Work and a Senior Research Fellow with the Traumatology Institute, College of Social Work, Florida State University.

I would like to thank George Blaha for conducting the qualitative interviews and Laura L. Myers for coding the interview transcripts.

This research was supported by a National Institute of Mental Health grant to Dr. Thyer (MH-12345). Portions of this paper were previously presented at the annual program meeting of the Council on Social Work Education, San Francisco, CA, October 2007. Conflicts of interest: none.

Correspondence concerning this article may be addressed to Bruce A. Thyer, PhD, College of Social Work, Florida State University, Tallahassee, FL 32306 or via e-mail at Bthyer@fsu.edu.

tables to report quantitative or qualitative data that are too dense to report narratively in an intelligible manner. A general guide is to report six or more bits of data in a table and fewer than this in the text as narrative. Do not, for example, prepare a separate table to report only the gender distribution of two groups of clients. But if you have several demographic characteristics (age, race, gender, etc.) for two or more groups, these may be best presented in a table. If in doubt, report the information narratively in the text. Tables are more expensive to publish than text, and since each table takes up one page, if the journal you are planning to submit your paper to imposes strict page limitations (15 to 20 manuscript pages, all-inclusive, is a common limit), keeping your tables to a minimum will help you adhere to these page limits.

Learn the APA guidelines regarding the formatting of tables and follow their minimalist standards exactly. Sometimes authors try to do the typesetter's job by adding to the table all kinds of fancy formatting, **bold** font, varying typefaces of differing sizes (including itty-bitty type to cram in tons of information), margins and borders, etc. Please do not do this. It will likely all be stripped away by the copy editor, who will curse you under his or her breath for adding to the workload. Make sure your table is double-spaced, has a brief but explanatory title, and is referred to in the text. In earlier versions of APA style, when one mentioned a table in the text, one inserted a note to the copy editor about where to place the table when typesetting the manuscript:

Insert Table 1 about here

It is important for you to realize that this is no longer APA style. Do not do this (unless your targeted journal's guidelines ask you to—some do). Simply refer to Table 1 in the text and add a note such as (insert Table 1 about here), or simply say, "as shown in Table 1." Each table mentioned in the text should of course appear, in order, after the references, and every table appearing after the references must be appropriately referenced in the text. The numbering of tables as presented in the text and appearing in the manuscript after the references must correspond. If you refer to Tables 1, 2, and 3 in the text, then Tables 1, 2, and 3 should appear, one per page, after the references. Do *not* insert tables in the text where you think they should go. Tables do not go in the text: they are placed in the manuscript *after* the references. Use only black-and-white composition in preparing your tables; few social work journals allow tables to be published in color.

Figure Caption Page

Sometimes you may wish to include a figure or even a photograph in your research paper. Do this very judiciously, if at all, knowing that figures, like tables, go one per page, and this can quickly chew up your page allocation. Figures can consist of pie charts, line graphs, scatter plots, regression curves, photographs, bar graphs, charts, maps, drawings, etc. Nowadays, figures usually must be submitted in electronic form rather than sent to the editor as hard copies along with the paper, so be prepared to scan your own figure if need be and have it ready to send electronically. Captions or titles must not be included as parts of the figures. These go on a separate page (the first one following the last table), and if you have more than one figure (and figure caption) you can list all the figure captions on this one page. Figure captions, like article and table titles, need to be succinct and convey essential information. Here is how they are formatted:

Figure Caption Page
Figure 1. Client satisfaction scores as a function of clinical social worker theoretical orientation.
Figure 2. Distribution of new cases of HIV across 30 Georgia counties during 2008.

Center the title "Figure Caption Page" on a new page, under the usual header and page number, then add the figure captions, as formatted above, noting the use of italics and capitalization. If a caption is more than one line long, the second and later lines should be set flush left.

After the figure caption page, what do you think comes next? Yes, figures!

Figures

As with tables, use figures very judiciously, if at all, and submit each figure on its own page. Seriously consider whether the information can be adequately conveyed using a table or as part of the narrative text. Avoid figures that present just a couple of bits of information (e.g., a bar graph depicting the mean ages of two groups of clients, or a pie chart with three divisions); instead, report this simple level of information in the text. When preparing your figures, avoid the use of color or even subtle gradations of black and white, as they may be difficult for readers to discriminate. Envision a pie chart with 10 divisions in varying shades ranging from white to black, with lots of subtle gray wedges. This could be very hard to read. Consider using different patterns instead (dots, cross-hatching, etc.) to distinguish your pie shapes or bars on a bar graph.

Some computer programs allow you to present your bar graph or histogram using a two-dimensional or three-dimensional format. Use two dimensions. Although the three-dimensional format may look prettier, it frequently does so at the expense of accuracy. Tracing the data back to the vertical axis when the graph has been drawn to look as if it were projecting from the page inhibits precise visual placement by the reader. Limit your use of three-dimensional drawings or diagrams to information that legitimately incorporates three dimensions, as in depicting a solid shape. Social work professor Mark Mattaini (1993) has prepared an excellent book called *More than a Thousand Words: Graphics for Clinical Practice* that is all about presenting data in visual formats; it is most highly recommended for those seeking guidance on this topic.

Well, we are almost done! Once you have completed each of the above sections of your paper, you have completed what is technically known as the first draft. It is a very good thing indeed to have a completed first draft, since revising existing material is usually a bit less taxing than composing the initial text. At this point, save your file, back it up to a jump drive, switch off the computer, turn out the light to your office, and go home and get some sleep.

Revising

Very few social workers can write a social work research article and have a finished product at the end. Almost all of us require a period of assimilation and revision of the first draft before we have a version we consider pretty good—almost ready, in fact, for submission. If time permits, run it through your word processor's spelling and grammar checkers one more time. Check its properties to see that you have no 50-word sentences. If you do, break them up. Then print out a copy and go over it at your leisure. Many of us prefer to edit from a hard-copy manuscript; others appreciate the ease of making changes on the screen. Use whatever method works best for you.

If you have any co-authors, you must allow them time to edit the work as well, and allow time for you to digest their suggestions and comply with them or come to an agreement regarding text revisions. All authors must accept ownership of the paper and agree that they are responsible for it. Everyone should agree as to who the corresponding author will be. *You* should assume this role if at all possible, since you know that you will conscientiously follow through on journal-related correspondence and answer any queries, and you can't be as certain that your co-authors will be so scrupulous.

A common nightmare is that you send your first draft to your co-authors and ask them to get back to you with any suggestions or changes right away—and then you hear nothing. Time passes. The manuscript rests. You send a reminder. And you get back nothing. Of course your colleagues are busy, and if they are senior to you, you may resist pressing them. But after a reasonable time goes by, their refusal to get back to you, or at the very least to give you permission to submit the paper, begins to impinge upon your rights and obligations. One good way to handle this is to send your colleagues the paper via e-mail, as an attachment (perhaps you can request an automatic e-mail confirmation that they have received it), and ask them to get back to you with any changes within some reasonable period of time, say 2 weeks. But tell them clearly that if you do not hear from them within 2 weeks, you will assume that they found the paper satisfactory, and that at that time you will go ahead and submit it to such and such a journal. It can be a little dicey to do this, depending on who your co-authors are (your dean versus your graduate assistant, for example), but it can be a good technique for dealing with laggard colleagues.

It can be helpful to have your paper read by colleagues or graduate students apart from your co-authors to get their feedback and impressions. It can be difficult to accept feedback that indicates that your project represents anything other than sublime perfection, but put your ego aside, listen carefully to what constructive remarks your readers may have, and consider the merits of their suggestions. Occasionally you will encounter genuinely helpful ideas that improve your paper. And if they make what strike you as idiotic remarks indicating that they failed to grasp the simplest elements of your design, keep in mind that your peers are probably a bit brighter than the average journal reader, and if your colleagues have trouble understanding it, you had better consider making things a bit clearer. I did not say that you should "dumb down" your paper; just make it clearer.

Proofing your manuscript one final time prior to submission is very important. Not all of us are good editors of our own work. You cannot catch everything yourself, but if your manuscript contains typos, grammatical errors, transpositions, etc., it will raise concerns among the reviewers of your work that the substantive content and data analysis may contain similar flaws, or errors of greater substance than a simple misspelling. To the extent possible, submit a manuscript free from such mistakes. As a test of your proofing skills, I have deliberately inserted a few mistakes into the typesetting of the present book. You can rest assured that these are not oversights or due to carelessness but reflect a conscious effort on my part to help you hone your proofing skills. And if you believe this, I have some waterfront property in Florida to sell you!

4

Submitting the Manuscript

Now that you have properly prepared your research article and chosen the journal you wish to submit it to, the next major task is sending it to the designated journal. There are two major ways in which this can be done. Increasingly, journals (and their publishers) are constructing Web-based submission portals that authors are required to employ. These Internet submission portals have many virtues, not the least of which being that by following a standardized protocol for entering all the information, you can be assured that nothing essential was omitted in your submission. For example, these sites typically require you to enter a corresponding address, e-mail address, and perhaps a phone or fax number for every author; to designate someone as the corresponding author for purposes of processing the manuscript through production; to provide the all-important keywords (later used by indexing and citation services); etc. This is good, but it can be frustrating if the Web portal is insufficiently user-friendly. For example, a good site tells you exactly what items are incorrect or missing rather than simply giving you a message that a submission is incomplete. A good site allows you to freely scroll through all pages of required information, even if you have not filled them out, so you can be familiar with the site's layout.

A bad site allows you, say, to move to item 5 if and only if item 4 has been properly completed.

Some sites require separate entries for your title page, abstract page, text, tables, figures, etc. Others allow you to upload a complete manuscript all in one piece. The latter is far more user-friendly, of course. Once you complete your entry your article will be assigned a manuscript number, and you should receive, via e-mail, a formal acknowledgment of your submission. In due course you will be informed of the reviewers' decision.

Other journals (a dwindling few) may require you to submit your paper as an e-mail attachment, with Microsoft Word documents being the most commonly required format. Fewer still ask that you send the editor four to six hard copies, and perhaps a diskette containing your paper. This latter scheme induces the most delays, what with the vagaries of postal mail and staff tardiness.

Regardless of how you submit your article, it should be accompanied by a formal letter of submission. The APA manual tells you what should be included in this, such as your postal address, e-mail address, telephone and fax numbers, and a clear statement that "the manuscript is original, not previously published, and not under concurrent consideration elsewhere" (APA, 2001, p. 382). If you have published similar manuscripts, especially if these used the same data set as this new submission, you should also proactively disclose this in your letter, with citations. It is also a nice touch to state that your study was conducted in a manner consistent with the APA or NASW Code of Ethics, reinforcing what you say in this regard in the manuscript itself. This letter of submission should accompany your manuscript. Web-based submission portals will have a place for you to attach it or insert it in a text box using cut-and-paste features. If you send your paper to the editor as an e-mail attachment, send along the submission letter as well; the same thing goes for hard copies sent via postal mail.

Your letter should be succinct, including the required information and not much else. Your submission letter is no place to praise the editor for his or her masterful service in editing this magnificent journal; to commend the editor's prior publications, which have proved to be so influential in your own career development; to claim to be a former student of the editor; or to otherwise schmooze the editor.

Conflicts of Interest

Increasing attention is being given in the scientific literature to the disclosure of real or potential conflicts of interest pertaining to your work (e.g., Krimsky & Rothenberg, 1998). Although such conflicts are more common in pharmaceutical research, where the industry funds researchers who are evaluating new drug claims, there are still opportunities for your social work research projects to conflict with your other personal or financial interests. For example, a social worker could help evaluate and publish an outcome study on virtual reality equipment used in psychotherapy. If the equipment were a commercial product and the social worker owned stock in the company, or if the manufacturer had (generously) paid the social worker for his or her evaluation expertise, more than the appearance of a conflict arises. Some journals require manuscript authors to submit statements relating to such possible conflicts of interest or to reveal them in a footnote to the published article itself. Some social workers earn large sums of money giving training workshops on novel forms of therapy they themselves invented. If such persons were involved in the design and publication of outcome studies on these novel forms of treatment, this too would present a possible financial conflict of interest. Or, a social work author may have written a self-help book for persons with a particular problem. If that author in turn evaluated the efficacy of this self-help book, similar issues would be raised. The APA manual says we should state, in a footnote to our paper where we make any acknowledgments, "any relationships [that] may be perceived as a conflict of interest (e.g., if you own stock in a company that manufactures a drug used in your study)" (APA, 2001, p. 204).

Use common sense here. If your retirement account includes a mutual fund that has some pharmaceutical stocks in its portfolio, that would not usually be seen as a conflict of interest and need not be disclosed.

Avoid "Salami Science"

"Salami science" refers to spreading out the numbers of articles derived from a single study to the denominator of the "least publishable unit." For example, I know of one doctoral dissertation involving the evaluation of a psychosocial intervention for the caregivers of people with a particular, serious problem. The caregivers' problems were assessed using two different outcome measures within the context of a simple pretest–post-test group design. After receiving a PhD, this author wrote one article for a journal describing the apparent effects of the program on one of the two outcome measures and sent an entirely separate article to another journal describing its effects on the second outcome measure. This is a good (bad?) example of salami science—stretching out the numbers of publications from your research project into as many articles as possible. Salami science may occur because a social work researcher perceives pressure to publish from his or her employer (e.g., a university), for reasons of simple narcissism, or to inflate the reputation of one's institution (if it is seen as the source of numerous articles, it can be seen as a more prestigious place). It is not exactly outright fraud, but it is very much frowned upon, as it is seen as inflating vitae and distorting the P & T process; it may mislead readers' sense of the true levels of research evidence about a particular intervention, it may complicate others' undertaking meta-analyses, and it wastes the time of editors and reviewers, among other problems (see Yank & Barnes, 2003).

It is apparently not an uncommon practice, though, and it is ever so easily slid into. For example, it is probably legitimate to use the huge literature review from your dissertation as the basis of a review article for journal A and to use the actual research results of your dissertation, with a greatly truncated literature review, as the basis of a separate paper submitted to journal B. A good litmus test is to ask yourself if you properly cite other papers derived from the given research project. If the answer is no, then the likelihood may be high that you are engaging in salami science and that you are trying to hide redundant publications.

One's doctoral dissertation may lend itself to several legitimately distinctive publications, however. For example, most dissertations begin with a thorough review of prior literature. Many journals regularly publish such literature reviews, especially if they provide some degree of critical analysis of the individual studies described. Hence your first chapter or two may lend themselves very naturally to a review article. Then a second paper may be crafted from your actual research study and its results. This would not be construed as salami science. It is also common for a novice postdoc to attempt to reduce a very lengthy dissertation into a single article, one containing a long literature review as well as a report of an individual research project. Keep in mind that many journals have page limits on their submitted manuscripts, and the ambitious, 50-page article condensed from your dissertation may be turned down out of hand by the editor of a journal with a limit of 20 pages for its submissions.

Salami science is not the same as publishing the same paper twice— that is a much more conspicuous example of fraud. The two papers submitted by the same author and based on the same outcome study, mentioned above, that are just reporting the outcomes separately for each dependent variable—that, too, is a pretty blatant example of redundant publication. There is no sound scientific reason for creating two publications in this manner when it would clearly have been the better practice to report both outcome measures in the same paper. But there was no fabrication of data involved, no bogus reporting; it is just the teeny issue of not citing one's earlier publication in the second one that creates the ethical problem. The study of academic and scholarly misconduct is its own unique field (e.g., Decoo, 2002). Social workers who adhere to the ethical codes of the National Association of Social Workers or of the American Psychological Association relating to scholarly research will not likely encounter problems of this nature.

5

Dealing with Revisions
and Rejections

The really successful authors of social work research articles have something in common: they all have had their work rejected at various points in time. Rejection is a fact of life in the world of scholarly publishing. It is painful and it is unpleasant, but it is the price you pay for entering the field and playing the game. In order to score touchdowns, you must take a lot of hits. Or to put it another way: in order to find your prince, you have to kiss a lot of toads. You must learn not to take the rejection of your paper personally. It is a part of our business. Even the best, most distinguished social work researchers get rejected all the time. If, as my psychodynamic colleagues put it, you are susceptible to narcissistic injury, either don't expose yourself to this risk or find a good behavior therapist to desensitize you to this experience!

In some ways it is easier to deal with a rejection than a request to revise your work. If, as too often happens, the letter of rejection is not accompanied by any peer reviews or critical commentary for you to consider, take the time anyway to review your manuscript one more time. Then, when you have it as near to pristine as possible, submit it to your second-choice journal. Continue *ad libitum* (as needed) to your third choice journal, etc. Do persist in this effort. I have patiently waited for several years and gone through a number of journals before obtaining eventual acceptance for more of my articles than I care to count. The advice that introduced this chapter should be followed religiously. I believe that this is especially true with research papers that you have co-authored with colleagues or graduate students, who may be depending upon your careful follow-up to ensure that their hard work pays off.

Now, you may object by saying that the repeated rejection of your article means that it really is a poor-quality piece of research and that you should abandon this effort. I assume, however, that from the outset your own professional judgment tells you that the work is worthwhile. I am not suggesting that you continuously send rubbishy articles out for review, but you need to balance your own dispassionate appraisal of what you have written with the judgments implied by or actually expressed in the letters of rejection. If you truly believe your work has merit, then keep at it. Console yourself by reading empirical research studies that examine the fate of articles published in a given journal and then later retyped by a third party and resubmitted to that same journal, in an examination of the test–retest reliability of the editorial decision-making process (Peters & Ceci, 1982). A surprisingly large percentage of these resubmitted articles were never identified by the editor as re-submissions of previously published works, and a surprisingly larger percentage were later rejected by the blind reviewers as unworthy of publication in the journal that had recently published that same article! What this means is that to some unknown extent, the editorial review and decision-making processes used by scientific journals are probabilistic. So even research articles found worthy of publication on one round of reviewing can be found unworthy at the second iteration. Journal editors and reviewers can have good and bad days just like anyone else, and most likely different reviewers would have ended up appraising these resubmitted articles. So rejection does not automatically mean that your research paper is of inherently low quality (or that accepted ones are of good quality!). Sad to say, the interrater agreement of reviewers assessing the same article at the same time can also be unsatisfactory. In a review of this topic, Kemp (2005) concluded that "the inter-rater correlations are not high enough to support strong statements about the value or quality of individual papers submitted. . . . The conclusion that good papers may be rejected (and, presumably, not so good ones accepted) is hardly new" (p. 782). Leading academic economists, including winners of the Nobel Prize, have had papers rejected, including some, subsequently published, that were later judged to be truly classic research articles (Gans & Shepherd, 1994)!

When your manuscript is rejected, you can perhaps find some consolation in these facts. But don't argue with the editor about his or her decision. Accept it graciously and move on. A postally mailed letter of rejection does not need a reply, but an e-mail is always worth responding to with a brief note thanking the editor and reviewers for their time and expertise. This leaves the editor with a positive impression of you and your professionalism, an impression that may help in the disposition of the next paper you send to that editor. Acting irate; arguing; and trashing the journal, the editor, and the reviewers are all usually exercises in futility. Accept the fact that we live in an imperfect world, move on, and send your research paper elsewhere.

If you get a request to revise and resubmit your work, this can be good news, since most conscientiously undertaken revisions that attend to the reviewers' suggestions will be accepted if resubmitted. Sometimes requested revisions are minor and easy to undertake and comply with. If so, count your blessings, make the revisions, and resubmit. Send along a letter with your revised research paper, and in this letter delineate how you have responded to the requests for changes. This letter should make the editor's job as simple as possible. If you indicate how and where in the paper you made the requested changes, this will save the editor time in reviewing your revision and put him or her in good humor. This is a good thing.

However, you are more likely to get some rather extensive requests for revisions, perhaps from multiple reviewers, and some of these recommendations may contradict one another! Here is how you should proceed: Label the reviewers as Reviewer A, B, C, and so forth. This can be done on hard copy, if you have been provided with hard-copy reviews, or on a word-processed document if you were sent requests for revisions electronically. Then, within each set of comments from the individual reviewers, label each substantive suggestion or indicated change as #1, #2, etc. Pay close attention to the first suggestion by Reviewer A. If it is sensible, comply with it and revise your paper accordingly. If it is nonsensical, ignore it and move on. If you have a legitimate reason to disagree with it, make a choice to forego your own preferences and comply with the revision, or to decline to comply with it. Then, in your cover letter detailing how you have responded to each substantive critique, indicate what you have done and where (e.g., "see page 3, second paragraph"). If you declined to follow the reviewers' suggestions, succinctly state your reasons for doing so. Sometimes it will be a matter of simple disagreement. Sometimes it will be due to the reviewer's inability to understand what you did. Sometimes the reviewers are simply wrong, as in a reviewer who recommends using a t-test to analyze frequency data or a χ^2 test to analyze ratio data. Explain why you did not follow the request in question. Continue this process for the entire litany of reviewers' suggestions. Address each substantive one, allowing the editor to see that you paid attention to everything. When your revision and accompanying letter are complete, resubmit your package to the editor and await developments.

As you do this, keep in mind the observation of George Orwell that "no passion in the world is equal to the passion to alter someone else's draft." Some reviewers are completely unable to resist "touching up" your paper. Do not expect sensible commentary from the reviewers; just accept that bending before their judgment is sometimes necessary, unpleasant though it may be, in order for you to be issued that coveted letter of acceptance.

6

Your Obligations as
a Published Author

Now, once you have been notified that your research article has been accepted by a journal, you may think that your task is complete, but this is only partially true. The majority of the effort—conceiving and designing the study, carrying it out, analyzing the data, writing up the report, preparing the manuscript, and finding it a scholarly home—is indeed behind you, but there remains some crucial and unfinished business that will require your attention both immediately and thereafter.

Celebrate

First off, pat yourself on the back. Notify your anxious co-authors of the acceptance and send them a copy of the formal letter of acceptance. Notify your boss, supervisor, or dean of your good news. If you have supportive colleagues, let them know as well so that they can share in the joy of your success. If your college or university has a publication that regularly lists faculty publications, be sure an announcement of your acceptance is sent to that publication. Take your spouse or partner to dinner. Enjoy a bottle of wine with your good meal. It is really a fine thing to have a good piece of research accepted by a high-quality social work journal, and you deserve lots of credit for accomplishing this. Now, back to attending to business.

Obtain, Sign, and Return the Author's Agreement

All publishers will want you to sign an author's agreement, which transfers certain rights to your work from you to them, in return for their undertaking the responsibility of publishing your masterpiece. The editor of the journal will likely send you the standard author's agreement used by his or her journal, either by postal mail or (more likely) as a PDF file sent via e-mail. If need be, print this first, read it carefully, sign it, and return it to the editor or publisher's office, whichever is indicated. Publishers may require an original signature, not a faxed or scanned one, on this agreement, and hence it usually needs to be returned by regular mail, but this practice varies. Keep a copy for your files. The agreement may be a one-page brief document or consist of several pages of dense type and legal verbiage, much of which you may not understand. If the journal is a reputable one published by an established firm, you can sign the agreement with few qualms. There is usually nothing unusual, secretive, or fraudulent about its provisions. It allows the publisher to publish your article, perhaps to reprint it in some future anthology, and to grant permission for others to use it in, say, a course pack or an edited book. You usually retain the right to use the article for your own purposes, such as including it in a future book you may edit or in your own classroom instruction (e.g., making copies of it for your students or posting it on your course Web site). The APA's policy is as follows:

> Authors who publish in APA journals are permitted to reproduce their own articles for personal use without obtaining permission from the APA as long as the material incorporates the copyright notice that appears on the original publication. (APA, 2001, pp. 341–342)

The bottom line is that if you do not sign the author's agreement, the publisher will not proceed to publish your research article. You may, in your naiveté, get back to the editor with a demand that certain provisions in the agreement be amended or deleted altogether, or that new ones be inserted—in other words, that the publisher prepare a customized author's agreement just for you. Good luck with this! These agreements are usually pretty standard and not subject to amendment. It is best to sign it and let it go.

If you have co-authors, you may be asked to obtain all their original signatures on the author's agreement as well and to see that these are returned to the editor. Some journals require signatures from all authors, which can be a real pain to obtain, whereas others require just one signature from a corresponding author who attests that he or she has authority to sign on behalf of all authors. Another, perhaps easier approach to getting all necessary signatures is for you to e-mail the author's agreement as a PDF attachment and ask each co-author to print it, sign it, and send it to you via postal mail. You can then assemble all these individually signed forms and send them in to the publisher in bulk. Legally, it really does not matter if the publisher has one form containing all signatures or several forms with one signature each, so long as each co-author has submitted a signed document to the publisher.

Correcting Page Proofs

Once the journal has the properly signed author's agreement(s), the publisher will move ahead with production. The manuscript will be assigned to a copy editor who will check over the formatting and make sure all references cited in the text are in the reference list and all citations in the reference list are properly mentioned in the text. Your figures will be checked and rechecked, not necessarily in terms of the appropriateness of your inferential analyses but to ensure that numbers called out in the text correspond with tables and figures, that decimal places look right, etc. These copy editors are not statisticians, though, and their checking is often superficial (Is the abstract too long? Have you submitted keywords?). Their duty, in general, is to tidy up the manuscript. At that point you may be asked, by e-mail or phone, to check some facts or answer some queries, and you may get a copyedited version of your manuscript to review. Once the manuscript is in good shape, the work is typeset and assumes the appearance of an actual journal article. At this stage the work is called a page proof.

The better publishers always provide you with an advance look at the typeset page proof, often sent to you via e-mail as a PDF document by a staff member known as a production editor. The page proof may have some further queries printed on it: you may be asked to update any citations that were originally submitted in your manuscript as "in press," or perhaps you omitted the page numbers in a reference to a chapter. It is always exciting to get the page proof of your research article. Check it over carefully, as this is your last chance to correct any errors, either original to your manuscript or inadvertently inserted by the copy editor or typesetter. Especially review your statistical reportage, the placement and numbering of tables and figures, and the position of decimal points, as these are more prone to mistakes than narrative text because they are harder to see, for one thing, and because they require statistical expertise to recognize.

If corrections are few, you can send them via e-mail to the production editor. If they are extensive, print out the PDF page proof and mark your corrections and changes in blue or red ink (something that will stand out). You will be asked in your written instructions to limit your changes to correcting errors in composition, rather than adding several paragraphs of addition exegesis or reporting a new means of statistical analysis. This is reasonable given the added costs of making extensive changes at this stage; by rights they should have been made during the copy-editing stage. So judiciously correct the page proof, and now sit back until the article appears in print.

Keep Your Raw Data and Databases and Share Them, If Requested

You know, of course, that the free exchange of ideas and information is an essential feature of scientific research, and paranoid possessiveness about your data is quite out of place. Authors of research articles are expected to keep their raw data (e.g., surveys, transcripts of interviews, behavioral observation data) safe and intact; the same is true for their databases and code books. The latter are usually easier to maintain, as the information can be kept (backed up, of course) on a diskette, hard drive, or flash drive. Why are you supposed to do this? Well, one reason is that some journals in the behavioral sciences ask you to deposit your data with them (I am not aware of any social work journals that require this), and some federal agencies that fund research require this of articles whose research they supported. The rationale is that since they were funded with public money, all the information they obtained should be in the public domain as well. But the most salient reason is so that you can promptly and courteously respond to other scholars who request access to your data. They may wish to recheck your inferential analysis, reexamine your data using a different statistical test, or perform some secondary investigations on the information you obtained.

This is all legitimate, and any such requests should be reasonably accommodated. You do not need to postpone your honeymoon in this regard, but you should oblige such requesters, assuming they indicate their legitimate scholarly purpose. Someone making such a request who is an obvious lunatic does not warrant a response that occupies much of your time. It may seem hard for you to comply with this obligation of scholars—after all, you labored many months, perhaps years, enduring hours of tedious work, to produce the SPSS database your correspondent is so cavalierly asking you to send him or her. But you should do it. You can charge for any costs you incur, but these should be legitimate and justified and not inflated so as to make a profit or to discourage requests for information.

Most social work journals say they follow the conventions of the APA publication manual, and it is important to realize that this manual is far more than a style guide for preparing manuscripts; it is also a detailed protocol covering many scientific practices, such as who deserves authorship on a research article, how peer review is conducted, the obligations of editors, etc. The APA manual has this to say about retaining data:

> To permit interested readers to verify the statistical analysis, an author should retain the raw data after publication of the research. Authors of manuscripts accepted for publication in APA journals are required to have available their raw data throughout the editorial review process and for at least 5 years after the date of publication. (APA, 2001, p. 137)

The manual goes on to assert:

> To permit competent professionals to confirm the results and analyses, authors are expected to retain raw data for a minimum of 5 years after publication of the research. Other information related to the research (e.g., instructions, treatment manuals, software, details of procedures) should be kept for the same period. This information is necessary if others are to attempt replication. Authors are expected to complete promptly and in a spirit of cooperation with such requests. (APA, 2001, p. 354)

There is more to it than this, of course, so you should familiarize yourself with the further details of this policy as outlined in the APA manual. Another reason, not often openly acknowledged, is that such requirements help to keep us honest. If authors know that they are expected to provide raw data and protocols to others upon request, it serves to deter scientific fraud and helps disclose it when such fraud occurs. Occasionally studies are published in scientific journals and it is later revealed that the whole thing was a fabrication—there were no clients, no patient records, no data, just an outright fraud perpetrated either for perverse pleasure at hoaxing the public or, more often, in the interests of vitae-padding and of artificially enhancing one's career via added publications. Fortunately, such fraudulent studies appear to occur very infrequently within the social work research literature.

One recent survey found that this APA requirement to share one's data was actually rarely complied with (Wicherts, Borsboom, Kats, & Molenaar, 2006). The authors made such a request of a sample of researchers who had published in recent APA journals and obtained the raw data only about 26% of the time. However, the infrequency of compliance by others does not relieve you of the ethical obligation to follow through on this implied agreement when you publish in a journal that adheres to the APA manual.

Make Copies of Your Paper Available

In the old days when I was a graduate student, following the publication of a research article authors would sometimes get postcards or letters requesting a "reprint" of their work—a professionally typeset and printed copy of the paper, identical in every respect to the published article. These requests often came from international scholars and from folks who read an abstract of the article in one of the abstracting publications and wanted to read the complete report. When your article was published you could order reprints of your work (for a fee), and for an extra charge you could order them with colored cardboard covers, which made them look really spiffy. However, we have moved from the age of the postally mailed reprint to the age of the e-mailed PDF article—a crueler, harsher, more efficient age, perhaps, but one more facilitative of rapid scientific communication. One still gets the occasional request from a fellow seeker of truth asking for a reprint or PDF of a published work, and one should, of course, fulfill such requests promptly. Some scholars do not have library privileges granting them free access to journal articles, so they may write you directly. If you have a PDF file, e-mail it. If you do not, see about scanning your published article and sending it to your needy correspondent via the Internet. At the very least, make a photocopy of it and postally mail it to him or her. It is the right thing to do, according to the canons of science, and who knows? You may earn good karma.

Proactively Promote Your Research Article

After your article appears in print, consider making a list of scholars within and outside of the social work profession who are active in the area that your new paper focuses on. Staple your business card to a hard copy of your paper, perhaps with a brief note ("Dear Dr. X, I thought you might find this recent paper of mine of interest. Sincerely, Your Name"). Slip this into an envelope and postally mail it to the distinguished Dr. X. Await a courteous and grateful reply, but expect nothing. Less effectively, send the Dr. X's of the world a copy of your article as a PDF attachment, along with a similar, more specific note in the body of the e-mail, so that they do not think that it is spam. The sooner you do this the better; you want all the Dr. X's of the world to be citing your work, and the earlier you put it in their hands, the more likely this is to happen. If they never come into contact with your fabulous study, they cannot possibly cite it. You are doing them a favor by saving them the trouble of having to look your article up. Again, you will likely hear nothing back—but occasionally you will, and sometimes Dr. X will indeed be grateful for your courtesy and will actually cite your study in his or her own forthcoming paper. Of course, Dr. X's citation may be a rather critical appraisal of your article and a harsh delineation of its numerous deficiencies, but that is the risk we all take in undertaking to publish empirical research articles. With the credit and recognition for a well-done study comes the potential for ignominy by unknowingly conducting a poor one.

Summary

- Sign and return the author's agreement promptly and without fuss.
- Respond to the copy editor's queries promptly and without fuss.
- Correct the page proof promptly and without fuss.
- Keep your raw data and protocols for at least 5 years.
- Share your raw data and protocols with legitimate scholars.

• Send copies of your article to those who request one.
• Proactively send unsolicited copies of your research article to scholars active in your area of research.

Concluding Remarks

Well, dear colleague, you have made it this far. I appreciate your perseverance and welcome your comments (sent to Bthyer@fsu.edu) on how adequately I have addressed various topics or which ones I should omit or add in any future edition. I sincerely hope that you find the suggestions contained herein helpful when developing your personal program of professional publishing. More importantly, I hope that they contribute to the enrichment of the social work research journal literature by encouraging more professionals like you to prepare and submit articles describing good-quality social work research. Now, on to the next project!

And he departed, and began to publish....
—Mark, Chapter 5, verse 20

References

American Psychological Association. (2001). *Publication manual of the American Psychological Association* (5th ed.). Washington, DC: American Psychological Association.

Barker, K., & Thyer, B. A. (2005). An empirical evaluation of the editorial practices of social work journals. Voices of authors published in 2000. *Journal of Social Service Research, 32,* 17–31.

Bennett, L. W., Stoops, C., Call, C., & Flett, H. (2007). Program completion and re-arrest in a batterer intervention system. *Research on Social Work Practice, 17,* 42–54.

Blenkner, M. (1962). Control groups and the placebo effect in evaluative research. *Social Work, 7,* 52–58.

Decoo, W. (2002). *Crisis on campus: Confronting academic misconduct.* Boston: MIT Press.

Fischer, J., & Corcoran, K. (2007). *Measures for clinical practice and research: A sourcebook* (4th ed.). New York: Oxford University Press.

Gans, J. S., & Shepherd, G. S. (1994). How are the mighty fallen: Rejected classic articles by leading economists. *Journal of Economic Perspectives, 8,* 165–180.

Green, R. G., Baskin, F. R., & Bellin, M. H. (2002). Results of the doctoral faculty publication project: Journal article productivity and its correlates in the 1990s. *Journal of Social Work Education, 38,* 135–152.

Holden, G., Barker, K., Covert-Vail, L., Rosenberg, G., & Cohen, S. A. (in press). Do social workers deserve better? An evaluation of journal coverage in *Social Work Abstracts. Research on Social Work Practice.*

Howard, M. O., & Jenson, J. (Eds.). (1999). Practice guidelines and clinical social work [Special issue]. *Research on Social Work Practice, 9*(3).

Hudson, W. W., Thyer, B. A., & Stocks, J. T. (1985). Assessing the importance of experimental outcomes. *Journal of Social Service Research, 8,* 87–98.

Justice, A. C., Cho, M. K., Winker, M. A., Berlin, J. A., & Rennie, D. (1998). Does masking author identity improve peer review quality: A randomized controlled trial. *JAMA, 280,* 240–242.

Kemp, S. (2005). Agreement between reviewers of *Journal of Economic Psychology* submissions. *Journal of Economic Psychology, 26,* 779–784.

Krimsky, S. D., & Rothenberg, L. S. (1998). Financial interest and its disclosure in scientific publications. *JAMA, 280,* 225–226.

LeCroy, C. W. (1985). Methodological issues in the evaluation of social work practice. *Social Service Review, 59,* 345–357.

LeCroy, C. W. (1994). *Handbook of child and adolescent treatment manuals.* New York: Lexington.

Leung, P., & Cheung, M. (2007). *Journals in social work and related disciplines: Manuscript submission information.* Houston, TX: Graduate College of Social Work, University of Houston.

Marsh, J. (Ed.) (1997). *An author's guide to social work journals.* Washington, DC: NASW Press.

Mattaini, M. A. (1993). *More than a thousand words: Graphics for clinical practice.* Washington, DC: NASW Press.

Peters, D. P., & Ceci, S. J. (1982). Peer-review practices of psychology journals: The fare of published articles submitted again. *Behavioral and Brain Sciences, 5,* 187–255.

Rosen, A., Proctor, E. K., & Staudt, M. (1999). Social work research and the quest for effective practice. *Social Work Research, 23,* 4–14.

Royse, D., Thyer, B. A., Padgett, D., & Logan, T. K. (2006). *Program evaluation: An introduction* (4th ed.). Belmont, CA: Thomson.

Rubin, A., & Babbie, E. (2007). *Research methods for social work* (6th ed.). Belmont, CA: Thomson.

Seipel, M. O. (2003). Assessing publication for tenure. *Journal of Social Work Education, 39,* 70–88.

Sellers, S. L., Smith, T., Mathiesen, S. G., & Perry, P. (2006). Perceptions of professional social work journals: Findings from a national survey. *Journal of Social Work Education, 42,* 139–160.

Shek, D. T. L. (in press). *Social Work Abstracts:* "Strong and Well-covered" abstracts or "Small and Weak" abstracts? *Research on Social Work Practice.*

Snyder, P., & Lawson, S. (1993). Evaluating results using corrected and uncorrected effect size estimates. *Journal of Experimental Education, 61,* 334–349.

Spinelli, M. (1997). Interpersonal psychotherapy for depressed antepartum women: A pilot study. *American Journal of Psychiatry, 154,* 1028–1030.

Spinelli, M. G., & Endicott, J. (2003). Controlled clinical trial of interpersonal psychotherapy versus parenting education program for depressed pregnant women. *American Journal of Psychiatry, 160,* 555–562.

Springer, D. W., Abell, N., & Hudson, W. W. (2002). Creating and validating rapid assessment instruments for practice and research: Part 1. *Research on Social Work Practice, 12,* 408–439.

Springer, D. W., Abell, N., & Nugent, W. R. (2002). Creating and validating rapid assessment instruments for practice and research: Part 2. *Research on Social Work Practice, 12,* 768–795.

Thompson, B. (1999). Improving research clarity and usefulness with effect size indices as supplements to statistical significance tests. *Exceptional Children, 65,* 329–349.

Thyer, B. A. (2001). What is the role of theory in research on social work practice. *Journal of Social Work Education, 37,* 9–25.

Thyer, B. A. (2005). A comprehensive listing of social work journals. *Research on Social Work Practice, 15,* 310–311.

Thyer, B. A. (2007). Social work education and clinical learning: Towards evidence-based practice? *Clinical Social Work Journal, 35,* 25–32.

Thyer, B. A., & Myers, L. M. (2003). An empirical evaluation of the editorial practices of social work journals. *Journal of Social Work Education, 39,* 125–140.

Van Rooyen, S., Godlee, F., Evans, S., Smith, R., & Black, N. (1998). Effects of blinding and unmasking on the quality of peer review: A randomized trial. *JAMA, 280,* 234–237.

Wicherts, J. M., Borsboom, D., Kats, J., & Molenaar, D. (2006). The poor availability of psychological research data for reanalysis [letter]. *American Psychologist, 61,* 726–728.

Yank, V., & Barnes, D. (2003). Consensus and contention regarding redundant publications in clinical research: Cross-sectional survey of editors and authors. *Journal of Medical Ethics, 29,* 109–114.

Suggested Further Reading

Browner, W. S. (2006). *Publishing and presenting clinical research* (2nd ed.). Philadelphia, PA: Lippincott Williams & Wilkins.

Day, R. A., & Gastel, B. (2006). *How to write and publish a scientific paper.* Westport, CT: Greenwood Press.

Holosko, M. J. (2006a). A suggested author's checklist for submitting manuscripts to *Research on Social Work Practice. Research on Social Work Practice, 16,* 449–454.

Holosko, M. J. (2006b). *Primer for critiquing social research: A student guide.* Belmont, CA: Thomson.

National Association of Social Workers. (2005). Peer review and publication standards in social work journals: The Miami statement. *Social Work Research, 29,* 119–121.

Pan, M. L. (2004). *Preparing literature reviews: Qualitative and quantitative approaches* (2nd ed.). Glendale, CA: Pryczak Publishing.

Pryczak, F. (2005). *Evaluating research in academic journals* (3rd ed.). Glendale, CA: Pryczak Publishing.

Pryczak, F., & Bruce, R. R. (2005). *Writing empirical research reports* (5th ed.). Glendale, CA: Pryczak Publishing.

Silvia, P. J. (2007). *How to write a lot: A practical guide to productive academic writing.* Washington, DC: American Psychological Association.

Thyer, B. A. (1994). *Successful publishing in scholarly journals.* Thousand Oaks, CA: SAGE.

Thyer, B. A. (2002). How to write up an outcome study for publication. *Journal of Social Work Research and Evaluation: An International Publication, 3,* 215–224.

Index